**NICK ELDRIDGE** UNIQUE HOUSES

# NICK ELDRIDGE

LUND
HUMPHRIES

DOMINIC BRADBURY

# UNIQUE HOUSES

# NEW

06 Introduction

20 Greenways, Coombe Park, Kingston, London

38 House in Epsom, Surrey

50 Beach House, Shoreham-by-Sea, West Sussex

58 House in Highgate Cemetery, Highgate, London

70 Cor-Ten House, Putney, London

82 Garden House, Highgate, London

# RENEW

| | | | | |
|---|---|---|---|---|
| 98 | The Lawns, Highgate, London | | 161 | Afterword |
| 110 | House in Belsize Park, London | | 170 | Practice Chronology |
| 120 | House in Chelsea, London | | 172 | Index |
| 128 | House in Hampstead, London | | 175 | Credits |
| 138 | House in Notting Hill, London | | | |
| 148 | Barn in Newlyn, Cornwall | | | |

# INTRODUCTION
# TAILORED DESIGN

'Private houses are so tailored to their owners that it makes each individual project very different', says architect Nick Eldridge. 'The design process is never repetitive and, without doubt, it is an area where it is possible to generate new ideas. Although a style may emerge across our residential work, there is never a formula. Each of our houses is unique and that is what makes our work so rewarding.'

Ever since 2000, when Nick Eldridge completed a house known as The Lawns in Highgate (see pages 98–109), his practice has been exploring the delightful sense of difference that makes each project original. As an architect and designer, Eldridge has worked on a broad range of typologies yet he has been drawn back to the architecture of house and home, for which the practice has become well known. The attention generated by the prestigious place that The Lawns secured on the shortlist for the Stirling Prize naturally opened up a world of offers and opportunities, yet every commission has been treated as a fresh beginning. These have included landmark new builds such as Greenways in Coombe Park (see pages 20–37) or the House in Highgate Cemetery (see pages 58–69), but also radical reinventions and reworkings of existing buildings.

For Eldridge, one of the most stimulating aspects of developing such a portfolio is the way that the architecture of house and home naturally spills over into other fields of design, such as interiors, furniture and landscape design. Over the last 20 years, the practice has taken pride and pleasure in regularly stepping across the borderland between these disciplines and adopting a multi-layered approach. In doing so, a particular passion for materiality and fine craftsmanship has become evident, as well as a focus on engaging architectural forms that – in themselves – suggest something unique. Yet, as Eldridge makes clear, such ideas only emerge in response to specific contexts and settings or from conversations and collaborations with clients, many of whom are also involved in creative professions.

'The design of private houses forges a special relationship between client and architect, as well as all those involved in crafting and making them', says Eldridge. 'The Lawns, along with being shortlisted for the Stirling Prize, really set us off down a particular path and put us on the

**6** UNIQUE HOUSES

map. But it was also quite a radical building in a Conservation Area that led to similar projects and clients in Highgate, Hampstead, Primrose Hill and areas where planning constraints required our approach. In some ways that project typecast us, and it can be difficult to break away from the work you are best known for. But given that, for me, residential design is always so enjoyable, perhaps that is not really something to worry about.'

i. BACKGROUND

Nick Eldridge was fortunate to know, from a young age, what he wanted to do with his life. As a child, his two greatest loves were art and music – singing in the choirs of Canterbury Cathedral and St Margaret's, Westminster, and successfully auditioning for a Scottish Opera production of Britten's *Turn of the Screw*. But it was in the art room at school where his attention was diverted towards a career in architecture.

'I had taken a keen interest in design as both my parents attended art school and our shelves at home were full of inspirational books of all kinds', says Eldridge. 'The turning point came when I was around 13 years old and my art master at school set us an architectural project with an open brief. The drawings and the card model that I made of an art gallery in Hyde Park, partially below ground, were well received. My parents were told that the project was worthy of a second-year architecture student and that I should be encouraged to consider studying architecture at university.'

Eldridge was born in London but the family moved to rural Kent when he was just four years old. The family lived in a Victorian house, but during the working week his father would commute into central London where he worked as an art director for an advertising agency. Eldridge's father was an excellent draughtsman who encouraged his son's sketching and drawing skills, but also shared an interest in art and design. His father and mother had first met at art school, where she studied textiles and nurtured an enduring love of dressmaking and tailoring, focused on craft and materials.

His parents furnished the house largely with antiques, with the family often heading off to antique shops at the weekends. This love of collecting proved infectious, with Eldridge developing an interest in beautifully crafted objects of design both antique and modern.

'It was a fascination with beautifully made things', Eldridge says. 'I would collect these pieces because I loved the look and feel of them and their material quality. Pieces of cutlery were interesting to me because they were also useful. I was drawn to undecorated flatware patterns of the early 18th century and later to the work of Danish silversmith Georg Jensen, with designs by the architect Arne Jacobsen and Svend Slune, who designed a range called Blue Shark in 1965 in heavy but well-balanced stainless steel. Jacobsen cutlery was laid out on my cousins' Fritz Hansen table, and we sat on three-legged Ant chairs also by Jacobsen. My uncle was a journalist in Fleet Street, who had an extraordinary design sense that had inspired me – yet regretfully we never discussed it.

'I think what appealed to me was the combination of function, form and materiality – and now, when I design something like a door handle for a house like Greenways, I have that sense of an opportunity to add a precious detail to the building that may well go largely unnoticed as it sits quietly in the overall composition.'

By the time Eldridge was 18, he already had a very clear idea of what he wanted to do and where he wanted to study. During his year off before heading to university he was not at all afraid to write to architects whose work he found interesting, often receiving generous and positive responses in return. He wrote to Michael and Patty Hopkins, for example, and was given a guided tour of their self-designed, steel-framed house and studio in Hampstead, now seen as an iconic exemplar of British High-tech architecture.

I remember walking along Downshire Hill past Victorian and Edwardian buildings and discovering the high-tech glass house. Crossing the bridge from the street, I entered at first-floor level, where I was shown around the house by Michael Hopkins. I had not yet started my training as an architect but I was aware of how beautifully and rigorously detailed this building was.'

Before university, Eldridge also managed to get a job with Chamberlin, Powell and Bon, the architects of the Barbican and the Golden Lane Estate. He spent two months helping to sort out the practice's archives and was then given some time, and encouragement, in the office. This job helped to fund time spent travelling in Europe and then a trip to Hong Kong, followed by Japan, where he was hosted by the family of one of his father's advertising clients from Japan Airlines.

'I was absolutely fascinated by Japan', Eldridge says. 'The family lived just outside Tokyo but what really intrigued me was the minka, the traditional Japanese house that belonged to one of the couple's parents on part of the site near to where Hiro and Fumi had later built their mono-pitched European-style house. After a week in Tokyo, I was put on the train to Kyoto and booked into a ryokan, a traditional Japanese inn, and Kyoto, with its wooden buildings and temples, was just magical. The depth of the Japanese tradition of architecture and crafts has had an enormous influence on my life and work.'

Back in England, Eldridge started his studies in architecture at Liverpool University. He felt the need to step away from London and from Kent, partly to gain a degree of independence and to spend time in a fresh environment. It was not so much the modern architecture of the city that captured his attention but the crumbling state of many period terraces in Liverpool at the time. As a student, his thoughts turned to regeneration and ways of bringing new life to these surroundings through architecture and design.

But, by the end of his first degree, Eldridge was starting to miss London and decided to return. He managed to secure a year's work with the multidisciplinary studio Pentagram, working under one of its founders, architect and designer Theo Crosby. It was another valuable experience, with Eldridge particularly inspired by the cross-fertilisation within the practice between the different design departments.

'The architects were on a mezzanine level overlooking the graphic and industrial designers, so just below us were Alan Fletcher and Kenneth Grange', Eldridge says. 'Although my father had talked about Fletcher Forbes Gill, I didn't know much about them when I joined but began to understand how influential they were in their fields of design. Much of the architectural work we were doing actually strayed into interiors, and Theo was occupied with bespoke designs working for corporations such as Unilever and at the same time helping Sam Wanamaker realise his vision for the reconstruction of Shakespeare's Globe Theatre on Bankside.

'We were kept in our little architectural bubble until lunchtime and then we would all go to the staff restaurant and mix with the other designers. At the end of the year, Pentagram allowed me to transfer to their studios in the Flatiron Building on Broadway and Fifth Avenue in New York. Here I met Colin Forbes, a co-founder of Pentagram, who asked me if I could prepare a set of working drawings to give to his builder for an extension to his ranch in North Carolina. I was living in a loft on Canal Street owned by a friend who had been introduced to me by a tutor at Liverpool. Sensing my nervousness about taking on the ranch project, she bought me a book on timber construction, enabling me to study the vernacular details and produce a set of working drawings.'

For a young architect, Manhattan, in itself, offered a wonderful microcosm full of design icons. Again, Eldridge began writing letters to architects that he found interesting and whose work he admired. In New York, he received a response from Philip Johnson, whose landmark AT&T Building on Madison Avenue was under construction at the time.

'I realised that as a young student you could write to famous people, like Johnson, and they would usually write a letter back or even agree to meet you', Eldridge says. 'The AT&T building was a towering concrete skeleton at the time and absolutely stunning. The entrance hall had large circular holes cut in the walls. It was all the more extraordinary because of my familiarity with his Modernist New Canaan house of 1949. The AT&T was the first Post-Modern skyscraper, and with age it was clear that Johnson had become more adventurous.

'Johnson made an impression on me. But far from being daunted in the presence of this man, I confidently showed him my portfolio and the glass house that I had designed in Liverpool between two derelict Georgian terraces. I explained that I would like to build it but it was obviously ambitious. He said, "Well, without ambition, you won't get anywhere."'

## ii. BEGINNINGS

Taking Johnson's words with him, Eldridge returned to London and seized another golden opportunity: working in the office of Norman Foster. He had originally intended to go back to Liverpool University, but a friend who was working with Foster suggested that he try for a job with the practice. It was the beginning of a highly formative period spent with Foster + Partners, which included the completion of his studies and his involvement with a number of key projects.

A plan developed with Eldridge deciding to pay his fees at the Architectural Association (AA), where he hoped to complete his studies, with his earnings from his day job at Fosters. To save some money, he took up residence in a geodesic dome that his father had discovered on the rooftop of the Fitzrovia office building, just off Charlotte Street, rented by his advertising agency. Eldridge's mother helped him with the design of the interiors of the dome, making a canvas skin for the inside of this Buckminster Fuller-style pod using triangular fragments of fabric stitched together; she also made bean bags for him in white PVC, creating a surreal rooftop escape accessible only by ladder on the outside of the building from the terrace below.

He enrolled at the AA in a unit run by architect and Pentagram partner Ron Herron, who had also interviewed Eldridge for his old job at the Pentagram studio, and Jan Kaplický, who worked with Foster before co-founding Future Systems. It was an unusual and demanding double act, with Eldridge fulfilling the many duties of his day job and then working during the evenings and weekends on his studies.

'I had to organise myself', says Eldridge. 'I needed to hold down the job and do well, but I also wanted to do well at the AA. I tried not to mix the two and just show dedication to the project that I was working on. When I joined, during the summer, Fosters were just finishing their Renault Swindon building and my first job was to snag the defects in the aluminium cladding from a cherry picker.'

It was, Eldridge suggests, the perfect time to be working at the practice.

There was a great deal of originality and invention but also plenty of opportunities, given that a significant part of the team was in Hong

Kong working on the practice's new headquarters for HSBC. It was also a time just before computer-aided design, with every plan done by hand in ink on Mylar drafting film – so Eldridge was able to hone his drawing skills, tutored by Kaplický. The buildings themselves were key examples of engineered High-tech architecture, comparable at the time only with the work of Michael Hopkins, Richard Rogers and Nicholas Grimshaw.

'There was much to learn', says Eldridge, 'and there were many talented people in the office to watch and learn from.' But because the team was quite small at that point I began to have direct access to Norman Foster, which is something you would not enjoy today. I was naively unaware of the office hierarchy and used to speak up in review meetings and make suggestions. I proved I could draw and started working on competitions for projects like the second phase of IBM Greenford, introducing some ideas. Eventually one of the directors took me down to the basement meeting room and said, "this office is democratic but not that democratic".

I escaped the hierarchy when Norman Foster sent me to France to manage his own house and studio project near Grasse.'

The house in France offered a chance to work closely with Foster yet it was – also – importantly Eldridge's first major residential project, with a highly discerning client in the shape of the architect himself. Foster had bought a large, stone-built farmhouse on a hillside near Grasse, dating back to the 18th or early 19th century. The mas was more or less habitable, so Eldridge largely based himself at the house while the work was being done – with Foster coming down every few weeks to go over what had been achieved and provide a new list of jobs that needed to be finished. Along the way, Eldridge was required to rapidly improve his French-language skills to a professional working standard.

'It was quite an intense experience because Norman Foster had very high expectations. The difficulty was that the builders were particularly difficult to organise and Norman would set a deadline on when work needed to be completed, because he would be coming down with the family for a holiday or people were coming to stay at the house. I would be trying to rally the French builders, plumbers and electricians to meet the deadline, so that part of it was very stressful.

'That summer I flew back to England to get married and had asked Norman for recommendations of places to stay in the South of France for our honeymoon. On my salary they were, of course, far too expensive but I nevertheless booked the hotel in Cap Ferrat and Château Eza, turning over the tariff on the back of the door so my wife Alison wouldn't know how much had been spent.'

The work on the house itself lasted around a year. Following on from its completion, Eldridge was asked to stay on in France and work on Foster + Partners' Médiathèque building in Nîmes, also known as the Carré d'Art; there was also the pleasure of living in Nemausus, an apartment building in the city designed by Jean Nouvel. He then managed to persuade his father to buy a ruined hamlet in the Luberon, a lengthy commuting distance from Nîmes, as a family escape – with Eldridge able to translate his experience on the Foster house into something more personal.

Yet by the point that he returned to the London office, times had changed. Much of the Hong Kong team had also returned, and the office seemed very different in character. There was also a feeling, after six positive years and being made an associate at the practice, that it was time to move on. He decided to apply for a post at the office of John McAslan and Jamie Troughton, now known as John McAslan + Partners. One of his first projects at the practice was designing the second office building for Apple at Stockley Park, West

London, marking the start of an eight-year period that spanned much of the 1990s.

One of the most positive aspects of Eldridge's time with Troughton McAslan was the breadth, as well as the depth, of the projects that he was involved with. There were, for instance, a number of large-scale infrastructure projects, including Canning Town Underground station on the Jubilee Line extension. Such commissions were ambitious not only in terms of scale but also in the way that they overlapped with engineering, both structural and civil. There were also cultural projects, competition entries and commissions in Italy and Turkey. Eventually, Eldridge became design director at the firm and, although they seldom worked together on specific projects, got to know Piers Smerin, another young architect and technical director.

### iii. INDEPENDENT PRACTICE

In many ways, the decision to launch Eldridge Smerin in 1998 was the result of both fortune and circumstance. Neither architect had nurtured strong ambitions to leave McAslan + Partners and neither seemed intent on refocusing, at that point, on residential work. Smerin had studied at the Royal College of Art and had also worked at Foster + Partners and with Zaha Hadid. Although Eldridge and Smerin shared an office at McAslan, they did not discuss founding a new practice together until the opportunity suddenly arose, out of the blue, to design The Lawns.

At the time, Nick Eldridge's wife Alison was working with the Design Council, and advising it on its move to new headquarters in Bow Street. Through this process, she got to know the designer and brand-identity consultant John Sorrell, who was Chairman of the Design Council from 1994 through to 2000. John and Frances Sorrell had recently decided to merge their own highly successful design studio with Interbrand, eventually

ABOVE The practice's first project: The Lawns, House in the Highgate Conservation Area. View from the south.

stepping back from the combined company in 2000, and they were just about to start work on a family home in Highgate.

'Alison had got to know John Sorrell through work, and he mentioned that he was looking for an architect because they were thinking of buying a house in Highgate', says Eldridge. 'I was just collecting my wife in the car from Bow Street and she said I should come in and meet John. Not long after that we arranged a meeting with the Sorrells.

'Initially, I think both Piers and I had the sense that it might be a project that we could do within the practice at McAslan + Partners. But the practice didn't really work on house commissions, and we started to realise that it wasn't going to work doing it that way. We hadn't talked about setting up a practice, but we began to think that if the project did come off then it would be a good stepping stone to starting our own studio – and perhaps there would be no option but to make the break.'

Given the success of The Lawns and the spotlight thrown upon it – and the practice – by the Stirling Prize nomination, a brave decision became a productive one as well. Eldridge Smerin marked a new beginning, with the attention generated by The Lawns leading to a series of residential projects across North London and beyond. The practice rapidly gained a strong reputation not just for the originality of its work but also for its persuasive and site-sensitive planning applications that were responsive to local contexts and the concerns of conservation officers in particular. Eldridge and Smerin took time to address the worries of neighbours and other stakeholders – such as the Highgate Society, which originally opposed the plans for The Lawns but eventually held its annual tea party in the garden of the completed house, kindly offered by the Sorrells.

The practice's respect for history and provenance carried through to relationships with architects such as the pioneering post-war Modernist John Winter, who had designed a house alongside Highgate Cemetery that was failing structurally and was eventually replaced by a new building by Eldridge Smerin. Winter himself was generous in his high praise for this exemplary 21st-century house.

Gradually, Eldridge Smerin began to win commissions for other kinds of projects that also informed the growth and evolution of the practice. There was, for example, the design of the Business & Intellectual Property Centre at the British Library and – in contrast – an entire floor of Selfridges Birmingham, with its distinctive outline created by Eldridge's former tutor Jan Kaplický and Future Systems. There were also commissions abroad, including the Villa Moda department store in Kuwait for which the practice had been recommended by Tyler Brûlé, the founder of *Wallpaper\**; *Monocle*; and Winkreative, which was responsible for the brand identity of Villa Moda.

Yet for both Nick Eldridge and Piers Smerin – who decided to set up a new, solo practice in 2011 – residential commissions had become the backbone of their portfolios. One project seemed to lead naturally to another, with a number of repeat clients and even – in the case of the Garden House in Highgate (see pages 82–95) and the Beach House in Shoreham-by-Sea (see pages 50–57) – twin commissions.

In 2011, Nick Eldridge was joined by associate director Mike Gibson, who had studied architecture at the University of Cambridge before spending a period of time working with De Matos Ryan. That same year, Eldridge decided to create two parallel studios, known as Eldridge London and Eldridge Newlyn. The West Country office is now based in one part of a converted barn with home attached (see pages 148–159). This dual structure across town and country has allowed the practice to spread its wings in more rural settings, with

ABOVE House in Highgate Cemetery. View from the west.

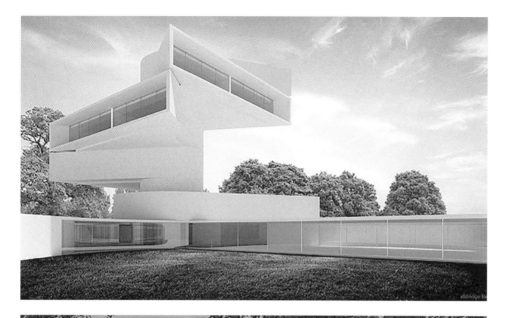

LEFT Paragraph 80 House in the Surrey Hills. View from courtyard towards entrance and pool. The bedroom floors above are designed to benefit from framed views of the open landscape beyond.

BELOW LEFT Paragraph 80 House in Surrey, now under construction. View towards the glazed entrance dividing the garage and guest wing to the left from the main house and pool to the right.

OPPOSITE ABOVE Interior view of the Modular, a single-storey pre-fabricated house raised on columns to accommodate different site characteristics, including sloping ground and flood plains. This option shows internal wood walls, floors and ceilings.

OPPOSITE BELOW Concept model of the Modular exhibited at the Royal Academy of Arts.

**14** UNIQUE HOUSES

commissions not only across the West Country but also in other parts of England, including Oxfordshire, Berkshire and Surrey.

The practice's noted dexterity with the planning process in urban settings has translated successfully into rural locations – working, for instance, on a number of one-off 'Paragraph 80' (formerly known as 'PPG7' and 'Paragraph 79') homes in rural locations where a successful application based on the 'country house clause' (as the relevant planning-documentation paragraph is also known) relies on a design of exceptional quality.

'With Paragraph 80 and its predecessors, you do learn that the planning process actually requires something extraordinary, which is an encouragement to us and to the client in terms of allowing time to produce an exceptional response to the site', says Eldridge. 'The project design is submitted to a Design Review Panel consisting of notable architects and landscape, ecology and sustainability experts to whom the Planning Authority will refer in terms of achieving the criteria set by Paragraph 80. It can be a lengthy and relatively costly process for the client, but rewarding when the outcome is successful.'

As well as these one-off houses, other rural projects have included the evolution of a concept system known as The Modular House, originally-shown at the Royal Academy Summer Exhibition in 2013 and developed further for a client in Devon. Making use of prefabricated components and standardised units, The Modular House offers an innovative approach to building rural homes that are both sustainable and affordable while still allowing for a degree of customisation according to the needs of the client and the site itself.

iv. THEMES AND VARIATIONS

Given the highly contextual nature of Nick Eldridge's work, in both town and country, it becomes a healthy challenge to try and pick out recurring themes and ideas across the portfolio. As we said at the very beginning, these are each bespoke buildings, after all, designed around a specific site and setting and also tailored to the needs and wishes of their owners. Yet, as the twelve case studies across the following pages might suggest, there are certain common threads that carry through both Eldridge's new builds and also the practice's reinvented buildings.

There is, for instance, a marked respect for the importance of the *promenade architecturale*, including the approach towards a building and the entry sequence. The practice generally favours entrance facades that are relatively enigmatic and abstract, posing a series of questions or mysteries about what lies beyond. The journey into and through Eldridge's houses, therefore, tends to offer a set of revelations and surprises as you are guided towards the light and the key views that gradually reveal themselves. Within this journey, feature staircases are a prominent focal point – introducing a dynamic or sculptural quality that might be juxtaposed with the more linear character of a room, or of the building as a whole. A great deal of thought and attention is given not only to circulation but also to establishing vibrant connections with the surroundings and relationships with outside spaces of one kind or another – whether a courtyard, terrace or roof garden.

There is always a rigour and a discipline to the design process that offers functionality and practicality, with a healthy provision of utility and storage spaces that then allow key living spaces to remain open and unencumbered. These are, in other words, houses that work hard while offering the luxury of open space. There is also a focus on craftsmanship and characterful materials that applies to both architecture and interiors throughout the practice's projects in town and country. We might tie this back to Eldridge's own background, with his early love of collecting or his time in Japan, and an appreciation of the important relationship between form, function, craft and materiality. This includes respect for the character offered by texture and patina, combined with an emphasis on fine finishes and detailing.

In terms of structure, the practice's buildings have always been ambitious and highly engineered, as might be expected from an architect with Eldridge's long experience at both Fosters and Troughton McAslan. But it is also important to note how Eldridge's houses have become increasingly adventurous and dynamic over time in terms of form. There is a fascinating energy to expressive projects such as Greenways, with its fluid form and sinuous lines. The same could be said of the practice's Barvikha House, which was designed with a series of floating cantilevered lenses pushing outwards from a circular core, or Stilemans in Surrey with its twisting white tower looking out over the rolling English landscape.

Such fresh and innovative projects point to the continued energy devoted to the consideration of more sculptural and original forms, but without repetition. In this respect, we are reminded of Eldridge's own comments about Philip Johnson and the way that original architects might become more adventurous with time rather than slipping into stereotypical solutions. Clearly, the ambition remains to explore new ideas and design solutions. 'There may be elements that suggest a signature', says Eldridge. 'But there's always the excitement at the outset of every project that anything is possible.'

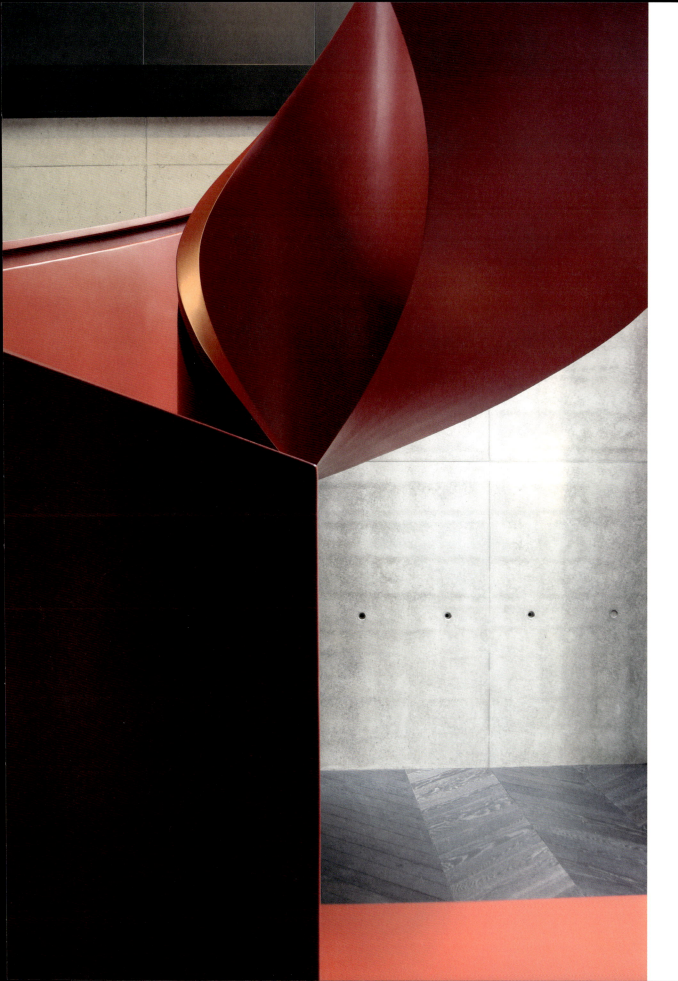

LEFT Helical staircase from the recently completed Garden House, Highgate, London.

INTRODUCTION 17

# NEW

Nick Eldridge's houses offer a delightful process of discovery. Purposefully, his buildings do not reveal themselves in an instant with a single moment of grand reveal. Instead, Eldridge tends towards an enigmatic threshold that marks the beginning of a gentle 'promenade architecturale' – the house gradually reveals itself and opens up as you are guided towards sources of light and open volumes.

The new-build homes featured across the next pages all offer special journeys of this kind, as they begin to unfold. The entrance to Greenways, in Coombe Park, for example, takes you to a crafted spiral staircase leading down to the lower ground floor, where the house opens up dramatically as you step into a spacious, open-plan living area looking out over the rear garden, including the mature trees that act as key points of reference for the project as a whole.

As seen in the following chapters, Eldridge's Garden House in Highgate, or his House in Epsom, offer experiences of a similar kind, where thresholds and transitional spaces lead towards moments of drama and surprise. But this is not to suggest for a moment that Eldridge's houses are all of a kind, because the opposite is true. Importantly, each of these buildings represents a highly individual response to a particular site, context and brief. These are tailored homes, crafted with care, which offer a rich and rewarding interpretation of 21st Century living.

# GREENWAYS
# COOMBE PARK, KINGSTON

With its combination of a dynamic sculptural form, highly crafted interiors and sensitive landscaping, Greenways is one of the most ambitious houses designed by Nick Eldridge and his practice. A key element within the realisation of such a rounded and characterful project, which was awarded the Manser Medal in 2017, was the creative collaboration between the architect and his client, who had cherished the idea of building a landmark modern home for himself and his family for many years. It was particularly helpful that Jim Mason is involved in the construction industry himself, and has an understanding of the design and building processes as well as an appreciation of modern architecture in general.

'I wanted a contemporary house and also to push the boundaries', says Mason. 'It's been an ambition for quite a few years and architecture is a passion of mine, so the intention was to build a home at some point. I wanted a house that sat well upon the site, and it needed to be discreet and private. But I also made clear from the start that this was a process that I wanted to enjoy and be a part of. I went to RIBA [the Royal Institute of British Architects] and told them about the project, and they came back to me with a list of six architects and Nick Eldridge was on that list. I developed a good rapport with Nick, and he suggested a scheme that I fell in love with. Greenways barely changed from that original design.

Mason bought the gently sloping site in Kingston-upon-Thames, complete with a 1950s bungalow, in 2012 with the intention of building a new home there. The setting is essentially suburban, with many of the neighbouring houses designed in an imposing neoclassical style although there are also a number of early modernist residences in the area. Having bought the bungalow, Mason then lived in it for five years while gathering the funds to build the new house. One of the advantages of this delay was that he was able to get to know the site

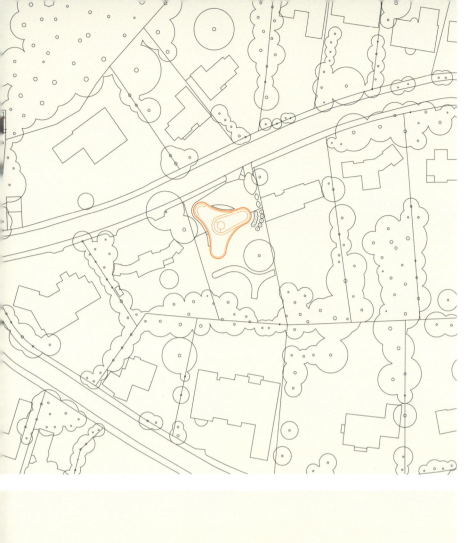

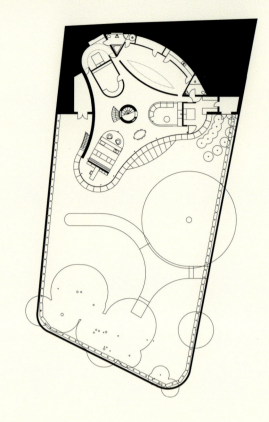

G

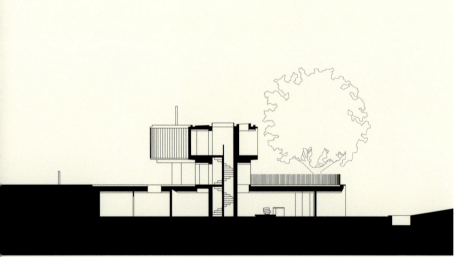

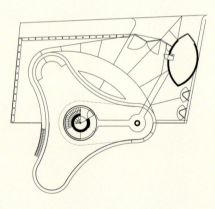

1

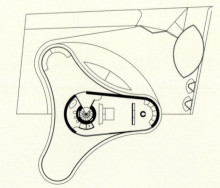

2

**22** UNIQUE HOUSES

PAGE 21 The master bedroom is supported on two columns above the trefoil-shaped ground floor living space with its curved glass walls opening onto the garden and oak tree, which generated the plan form of the building.

OPPOSITE Location plan, floor plans and cross-section showing access from the private road on the left to the rotunda entrance space leading to the living areas at garden level and master bedroom at the canopy level of the oak tree.

FOLLOWING PAGES View from the south with the natural swimming pond in the foreground. The water is filtered through the reeds and aquatic planting to the left, which also creates a tranquil backdrop to the study at this end of the ground floor. A guest bedroom on the right looks out onto a grove of elegant silver birch trees.

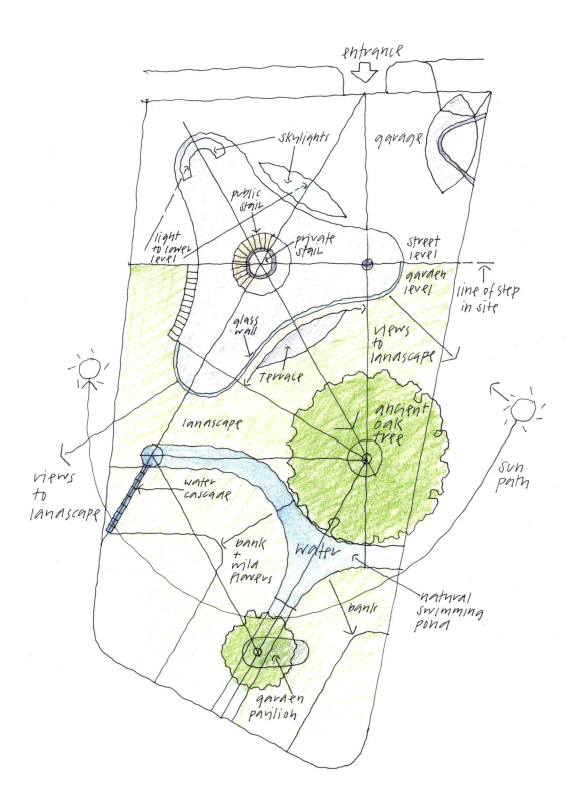

NEW 23

OPPOSITE View from street level towards the glazed entrance rotunda. In the foreground is an elliptical roof light set into the grass. Conceived as a reflecting pool in the landscape, this lets daylight and sunlight into the lower-level living space.

OPPOSITE BELOW The oak staircase from street level is suspended by brass rods and touches down at garden level providing a view of the garden and kitchen to the right with raised platform designed for relaxed conversation with the hosts at the marble kitchen island.

intimately – so that, by the time he met Nick Eldridge, he was clear in his mind that the house needed to both respond to and connect with the large rear garden, complete with its majestic oak tree.

'The oak tree was really the first generator of the curved walls at Greenways', says Eldridge. 'It's over a hundred years old and seemed like a good focus for the living space, which was the first of the curves that I set down on paper, and then we started creating repetitions of that first arc to create a trefoil shape. The trefoil then helped to divide the main floor into spaces with different functions, with the kitchen and study to one end, the living room in another and then a bedroom and media room in the third – with all of these spaces revolving around the central staircase.'

The design was contextually driven not only by the idea of connecting the key spaces to the grounds and the mature oak but also by the topography, with its sloping gradient dipping down from the access road and driveway at the front of the site towards the garden's rear boundary. The principal storey became the lower-ground floor, which has been pushed lightly into the slope while ensuring that the partially open-plan living area still offers a vivid indoor–outdoor relationship with the garden via floor-to-ceiling walls of glass.

The ground floor, then, became little more than a rotunda holding the main entrance and a double staircase, with an outer section leading downwards to the principal level complemented by a hidden inner section heading upwards to a spacious master-bedroom suite situated on the first floor. With its rounded edges, anodised-aluminium cladding and brise-soleil, this part of the house is an enigmatic 'floating' structure suspended high above the rest of the building – almost like a tree house. Such an arrangement not only offers a more energetic composition than usual but also establishes an intriguing contrast between the themes of elevation and excavation, with the void between these two distinct elements only enhancing the sense of drama.

'The only element that we really agonised about was the top floor and what form it should take', Eldridge says. 'My initial thought was that it could be a pure rectangle that then developed a number of iterations – including a long cantilever, which proved to be very ambitious from an engineering point of view and extremely costly. So we concluded with a rounded plan form with the curves at

PREVIOUS PAGES The sitting area features a curved sofa configured for views towards the garden. Beyond is the dining space, kitchen, wine room and the study, which can be closed off for privacy. To the right, the concrete core contains a private inner stair to the master bedroom and a separate outer stair to the entrance.

OPPOSITE The inset bespoke fireplace is made from brass and continues to the left and right as a band separating the meticulously book-matched Calacatta Oro marble panels from Italy.

each end geometrically determined by the column supporting it at one end and by the staircase structure at the other.'

Placing the master suite on its own at the top of the house offers a degree of privacy and seclusion, while the way that this floating element helps to frame, shelter and enhance the entry sequence below adds to the whole experience of Greenways' *promenade architecturale*. The procession from the entrance rotunda down the spiral staircase towards the principal level below offers a pleasing slow reveal, with the main living spaces and the garden beyond only becoming apparent at the journey's end.

Upon arrival, the luxurious character of the interiors becomes evident. The winding stairway itself provides the first indications of the overall approach to materiality and finishing within the interiors, with oak steps hung on brass rods varying in diameter according to their length while a matching brass handrail is fixed to the circular concrete core. There is an exacting level of detailing throughout the main living area, which holds the kitchen, dining zone and a sunken seating area within one fluid space. Reference points and influences here include hotels like the Sanderson and St Martin's Lane, where Eldridge and his client would meet to discuss the design of the house. The seating zone is arranged around a custom fireplace with brass detailing and a surround made of book-matched panels of pale Calacata Oro marble from Carrara, sourced on a dedicated trip to Italy.

'We were led by Jim's interest in more luxurious and expressive materials like brass and marble', Eldridge says. 'Having consulted a stone specialist in London, it was agreed that we would visit the Carrara quarry in Italy and with the assistance of a block buyer select two ten-tonne blocks – which would then be cut and book-matched to achieve continuity across the walls and floors of the two bathrooms together with a bespoke triangular bath and free-standing basin, also triangular in plan form. It was shipped from Carrara to Athens, which required a further visit to supervise the complex cutting, before it was returned as numbered pieces for installation. The CNC [computer numerical controlled] cutting of the bath from solid block was a remarkable process to watch.

'The triumph of this exercise was achieving these bespoke items for a price that was competitive with off-the-shelf elements bought in the UK. People tend to think that having something specially designed and manufactured means that

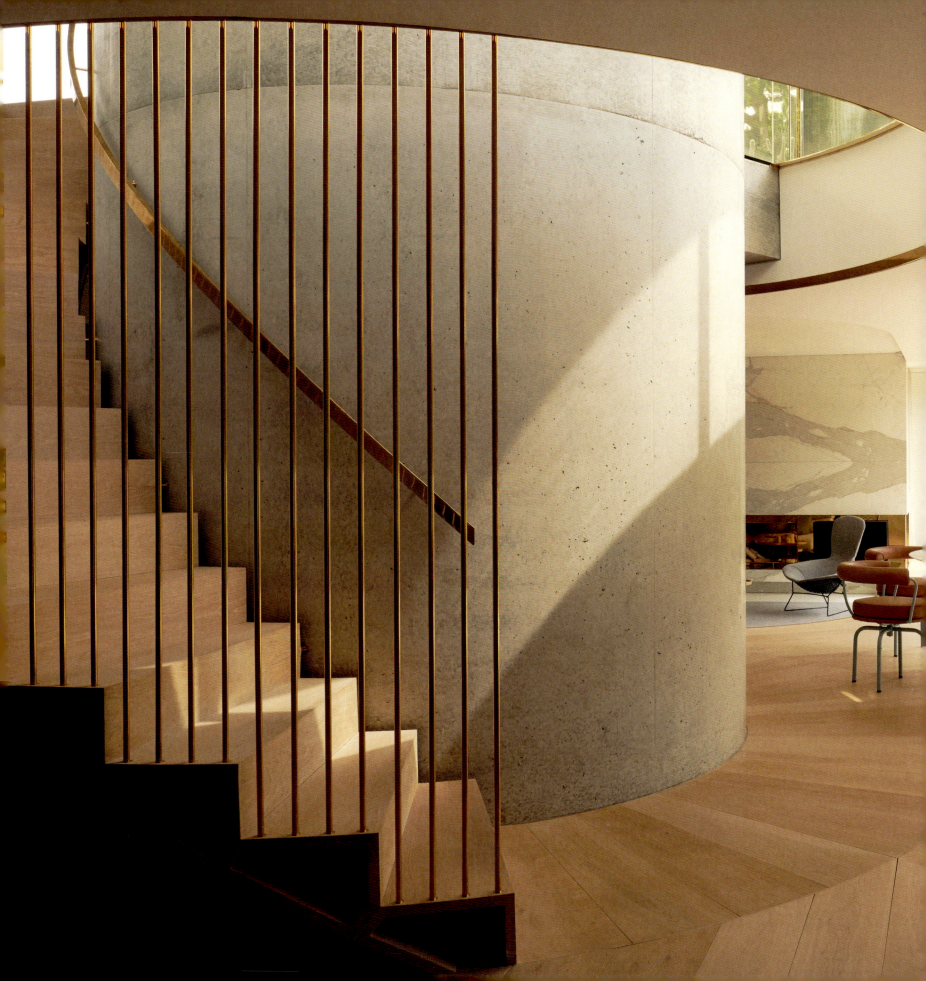

BELOW The bespoke triangular bath, wall and floor panels are book-matched and were cut from a block of Carrara marble sourced by the client and architect on a visit to the quarries in Italy.

RIGHT The private stair to the master bedroom is in oak-faced plywood. The in-situ cast-concrete walls of the core are washed by natural light from the oculus above.

BELOW RIGHT Door handles are in the trefoil plan form of the house.

it will always be more expensive, but that isn't necessarily the case as long as you are rigorous in your research and purchasing.'

The sinuous seating around the fireplace was custom-made by Coakley & Cox, while the kitchen alongside was – again – fully bespoke. Here, a marble-topped island doubles as a bar accessed by a slightly raised platform, while an elegant storage wall made with oak joinery holds a galley kitchen with a wine room tucked discreetly away behind it with a study beyond. The lower-ground floor also holds two separate bedrooms, a media room and a gym (now used, by Greenways' new owners, as a music room), with rooflights to illuminate spaces towards the rear of the plan. Curving lines continue through the house, with the trefoil pattern lightly referenced in details such as door handles.

'But you are not really aware of the shape of the house when you are inside it', says Eldridge. 'You know that there are curved walls of glass and concrete, but of course you never read the full shape of the house. So we have incorporated subtle references and reminders. The geometry does also mean that it is quite challenging to find furniture and other pieces that fit perfectly, which leads back to bespoke solutions. The project is, in a sense, an example of *Gesamtkunstwerk*, or total design, which we were encouraged to pursue by the client who enjoyed the uniqueness of each element of the design – from the scale of a door handle to the entire structural form.'

Another subtle reference to the trefoil comes in the design of the naturalistic swimming pond in the garden, with its natural filtration and purification provided by aquatic plants. The landscaping has also involved the introduction of additional trees, particularly around the edges of the site, to create a planted screen from the neighbouring houses. Such is the success of the positioning and orientation of the dwelling that, despite its location in Coombe Park, it almost has the feeling of a country home.

The Manser Medal jury described Greenways as a 'fantastically brave and well executed "grand project"'. Certainly, it is a building that stands out in comparison with its suburban context but also in the context of linear modernism. In many ways, the house and garden are reminiscent of the work of mid-century masters such as John Lautner and Oscar Niemeyer who broke away from the limitations of the International Style to explore more sculptural and fluid forms.

'Niemeyer and others were not conscious references for me', says Eldridge. 'But as a designer you do have these classic modern houses in the back of your mind, particularly works by architects that you admire, and Niemeyer is obviously a great point of inspiration that no one would be ashamed to list. But I would say that the sculptural shapes are primarily a response to the landscape. When we submitted a model of the building to the Royal Academy for their Summer Exhibition a few years ago, they exhibited the work in the sculpture gallery rather than in the architecture room, which reinforced my view that architecture should be regarded as art alongside painting and sculpture.'

For Eldridge and Mason, the creative process behind Greenways lasted close to a decade. It led not only to an extraordinary house but also to a friendship founded on a mutual appreciation of good design and high craftsmanship. Encouragingly for anyone with a dream of building their own home, it was – just as Mason initially hoped – a positive experience throughout.

'The whole thing was a pleasure', says Mason. 'Building a house can be really painful and I run a company that builds constantly, so I do understand that. But it was such an enjoyable thing to be part of and I think the finished house is outstanding. It met all my expectations and more.'

RIGHT At night the illuminated elliptical and crescent roof lights and entrance rotunda reveal the three-dimensional nature of the abstract design of the house at street level.

# HOUSE IN EPSOM
# SURREY

Along with a number of his contemporaries, Nick Eldridge and his practice have taken a growing interest in sustainability over recent years. Designing and constructing any new building carries with it a sense of responsibility towards the environment, but this is inevitably felt more acutely in sensitive settings and more open landscapes. The practice places particular importance on the way in which a house responds to its surroundings in a contextual manner, while searching for design solutions that mitigate the overall impact and carbon footprint of a new building. This can be a challenge in larger projects, such as this substantial family home near Epsom in Surrey, where Eldridge and his clients devoted considerable care and attention to a range of eco-sensitive strategies.

'It is a large house and essentially four storeys, if you include the mezzanine level, but also one of our greenest buildings in terms of energy use', says Eldridge. 'We have incorporated a ground-source heating system, with 80 metre (260 foot) deep boreholes in the garden, and solar thermal as well as a significant amount of insulation. It was designed at a time when there was a growing discussion about what architects could and should be doing from a renewable point of view, and the clients were also very keen on the idea of a green building. These kinds of solutions are now becoming more affordable and almost becoming a requirement. Certainly, if you want to design a glass-and-concrete building then you have to add in renewables to compensate.'

The setting for the new house is essentially the southern edge of Greater London, where the suburbs give way to the green belt. The site once formed part of the substantial garden to the neighbouring property, looking out over the open greenery of a golf course with views of Epsom racecourse in the distance. The architectural design of the new building needed to make the most of the views

40 UNIQUE HOUSES

PAGE 39 The formal entrance lies between the house and pool pavilion and its approach reveals a dramatic view to the golf course beyond.

OPPOSITE The double-height living space and bedrooms above are angled towards long views to the landscape.

RIGHT The pool is at the lower courtyard level for privacy from the golf course.

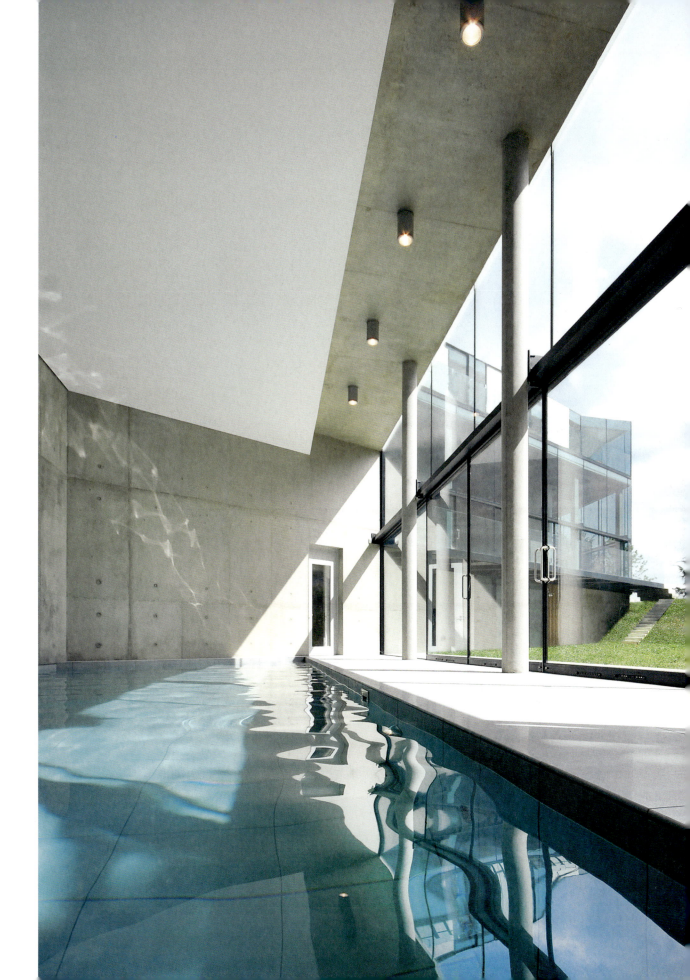

OPPOSITE Floor plans and concept sketch.

across this open landscape yet also ensure privacy from the neighbouring houses, as well as from passing golfers.

At the same time, it needed to accommodate the needs of Eldridge's clients, a family of four with two young children. The parents both work in the financial sector, and spent time working overseas before deciding to settle down in Epsom. The new house was designed with the children in mind, yet the practice's well-travelled and well-informed clients also carried with them a sense of ambition to create a fully tailored modern home.

'We all agreed that we wanted to design a house of great quality', says Eldridge, 'and the family were very supportive of that ambition. The clients actually undertook quite a lot of the procurement themselves, researching and negotiating for materials and products over the course of a three-year project to help create this large family residence of around 7,000 square feet [650 square metres]. They saw themselves living in this house for a long time, so it was an investment in their future and the idea of being in a setting where they could connect to the countryside but also commute into work.'

The practice's solution to the balancing act demanded by the need to ensure both privacy and connectivity was to orientate the house towards the golf course while creating a lower-ground floor complete with a sunken courtyard garden, sloping gently upwards as it stretches out towards the open landscape. The courtyard is partially bordered by the main body of the house itself but also by a projecting pavilion that angles outwards and hosts a swimming pool and gym. While offering the family a private realm, this solution also created a safe and semi-protected indoor–outdoor environment for the children while the lower-ground floor of the master building provides additional living space for a nanny and guests, as well as hosting 'engine room' spaces such as the plant rooms, storage and utility zones.

An added advantage of this arrangement is that it frees up the rest of the house, which looks over and across the courtyard towards the green vista. The ground floor, in particular, is a fluid and inviting family space with high ceilings; banks of floor-to-ceiling glass facing the landscape to the south-east; and an integrated, balconied terrace 'floating' over the courtyard below. Given that so many service spaces are tucked away at lower-ground level, this part of the dwelling feels open and generously proportioned with the reception area at one end, the

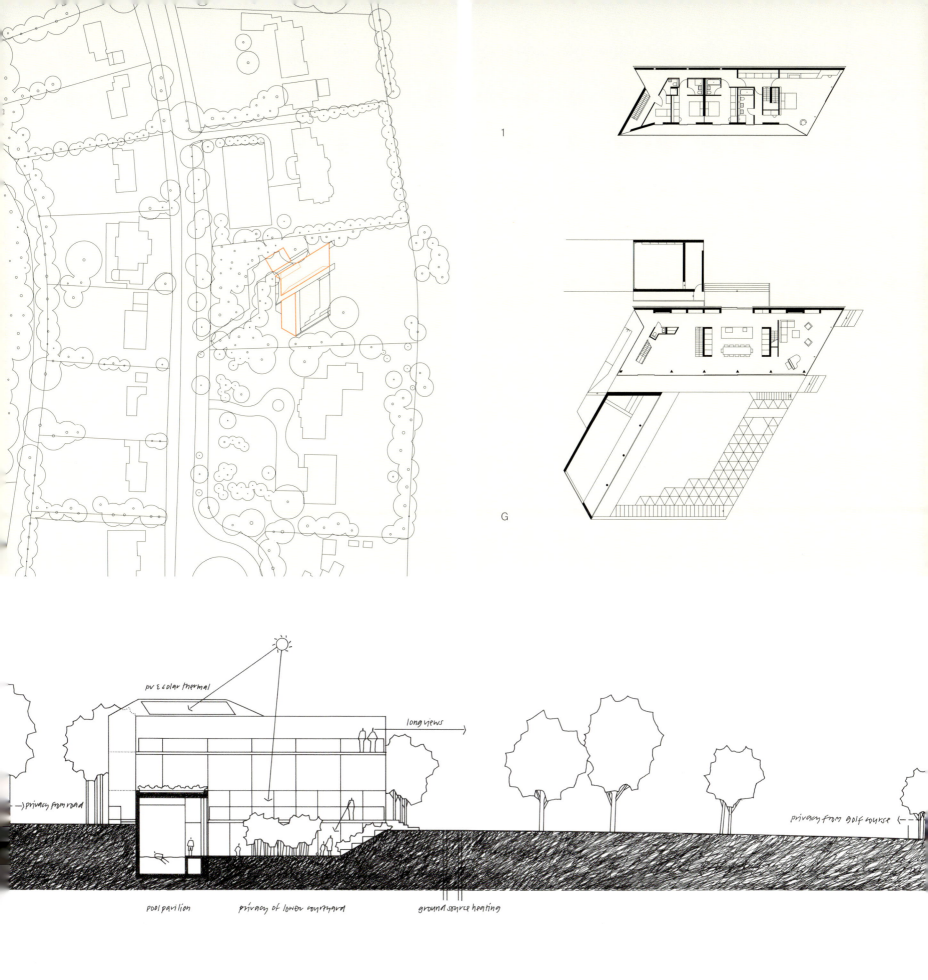

OPPOSITE The principle stair is made from solid maple and screens the five-metre-high living space from the road.

ABOVE The kitchen and dining space opens out onto terraces to the north and south. A mezzanine level above provides a more intimate family space within the double-height volume.

RIGHT Sitting room for music and views over the garden and to the golf course.

kitchen/dining zone at the centre and then the main living space beyond. Each of these zones flows freely into the next, lightly punctuated and partitioned by three staircases – each of which becomes an integral part of an installation that also holds storage and services.

Two of these stairways are discreetly concealed within these installations, with one leading down to the lower-ground floor and the other heading up to a maple-clad mezzanine – holding a media room 'floating' above a portion of the kitchen – before reaching the first floor. The third and principal staircase is a focal point in itself, while also serving as a pivotal part of the entry-and-circulation sequence. Visible from inside and outside the house, this feature stairway is a crafted element made with a vertical lattice of timber that forms a protective but semi-translucent enclosure around the staircase itself, while the maple also morphs into an elegant, L-shaped coat cupboard and cloakroom that offers a more organic element among the glass and fair-faced concrete surfaces of the ground floor.

'The staircase has echoes of Alvar Aalto's Villa Mairea [1939] in Finland, which I visited a few years before designing this house', Eldridge says. 'There's a wonderfully organic feel to that house and Aalto uses vertical wooden posts that relate to the birch forest that surrounds it. Here we sought a foil to the exposed, raw, concrete structural frame of the building, designing a staircase using solid maple treads and full-height vertical slats that are structural but also screen the entrance hall and living space from the road. Projecting from beneath the stair landing is a guest bathroom and coat cupboard that, in form, is a miniature version of the plan of the house and pool pavilion, and is designed and crafted as a piece of furniture elegantly placed within the double-height volume.'

The other point of inspiration here, Eldridge suggests, is Louis Kahn – whose Esherick House (1961) in Pennsylvania, for example, features similar contrasts between concrete and crafted timber joinery while exploring complex geometrical forms and ideas. With the Epsom house, a rectilinear plan has been subtly subverted in response to the site and sight lines, with angled walls and triangular shapes introducing a more dynamic and sculptural outline.

'The angular geometry of the house was emphasised by the unusual use of triangular concrete columns', explains Eldridge. 'These columns by virtue of their

OPPOSITE View from the mezzanine over the entrance hall with cloakroom pod inserted beneath the stair landing. The stair and cloakroom plan echoes the plan form of the house.

shape appear more slender than square columns of the same overall dimensions. When they were struck and the formwork was removed, we found they had a wonderful marble-like quality. Concrete cast in situ, however well managed, yields slightly unpredictable results, but the organic quality of the surface is part of the natural charm of this material.'

These angular elements and gentle surprises are repeated throughout the dwelling, including on the first floor. Here, three bedroom suites sit at one end of the house and a spacious master suite sits at the other, with all of these elevated spaces benefitting from the open views; a wealth of light; and access to a long, integrated terrace running along the elevation facing south-eastwards. Looking down into the courtyard below, the integrated and tiered planters that form part of the landscaping here also make use of triangular forms.

This is certainly a house full of thoughtful ideas, yet each one has been generated for a reason related to the site, the views and the needs of the family. Nothing, in other words, is superfluous – and every part of the residence and the enticing pool pavilion is put to full and daily use. For these reasons, as well as the originality of its design, the house was embraced by the planners and given a RIBA Award in 2011 as well as earning a place on the shortlist for the Manser Medal.

Returning to the themes of sensitivity and sustainability, the house also manages to embrace an original and imaginative architectural form while being sensitive to its neighbours and its overall impact on the setting and the surroundings. It is, in many respects, a discreet structure that is partly sheltered from the streetscape by mature trees and its orientation, while – as already discussed – the partial immersion of the building into the topography reduces its impact when seen from the golf course.

As an exemplar of ecological design, the Epsom house features not only a ground-source heat pump and heat-recovery systems but also solar thermal water-heating panels mounted on the roof. Low-tech strategies include the use of the concrete structure as a heat store and regulator, helping to maintain a steady temperature all year round. In the summer months, natural ventilation can be used to cool the house – particularly with the banks of sliding glass that open up on the ground floor. Such an intelligent mixture of passive solutions and renewable energy clearly sits at the heart of the future of the sustainable home.

ABOVE The clerestory glazing at the top of the house lets light into the first-floor corridor and the bathrooms with glazed ceilings. The north wall, which has limited window openings for privacy from the neighbouring house, also contains the vertical services distribution.

# BEACH HOUSE
# SHOREHAM-BY-SEA

Lying around halfway between Worthing to the west and Brighton & Hove to the east, Shoreham-by-Sea is an engaging and eclectic coastal retreat. The setting is certainly enticing – particularly Shoreham Beach, which sits on a slim ribbon of land and shingle with the sea to the south and the waters of the River Adur and the harbour to the north. The spit, by its very nature, has the escapist feeling of a half-way point between land and sea. During the early 20th century, Shoreham Beach grew into a micro resort known as 'bungalow town', revolving around modest homes converted from old railway carriages – as was also the case in places like Dungeness, further along the coast in Kent.

Much of the 'bungalow town' was cleared away during the Second World War, or shortly afterwards, with the post-war period seeing a fresh wave of beach-house building but on a larger scale. However, there was no dominant Shoreham style – leading to a broad mix of aesthetic approaches drawing upon a disparate range of influences, including neoclassicism and modernism. The combination of such engaging surroundings and a liberal approach to architecture, given this lack of an established 'house style', makes Shoreham Beach a tempting resort for 21st-century escapists who want to create a home of their own there.

Such was the case with Nick Eldridge's and associate director Mike Gibson's clients, who decided to build a waterside retreat to replace one of the 1950s build-ings. This new beach house was part of a twin commission, which also included the client family's principal home in Highgate, known as the Garden House (see pages 82–95). Yet the approach to the design of their Shoreham house is clearly and purposefully very different from that of their London residence – driven by the context, the need to connect with sea views and also a desire shared by both architect and clients to create a house with a uniquely escapist quality of its own.

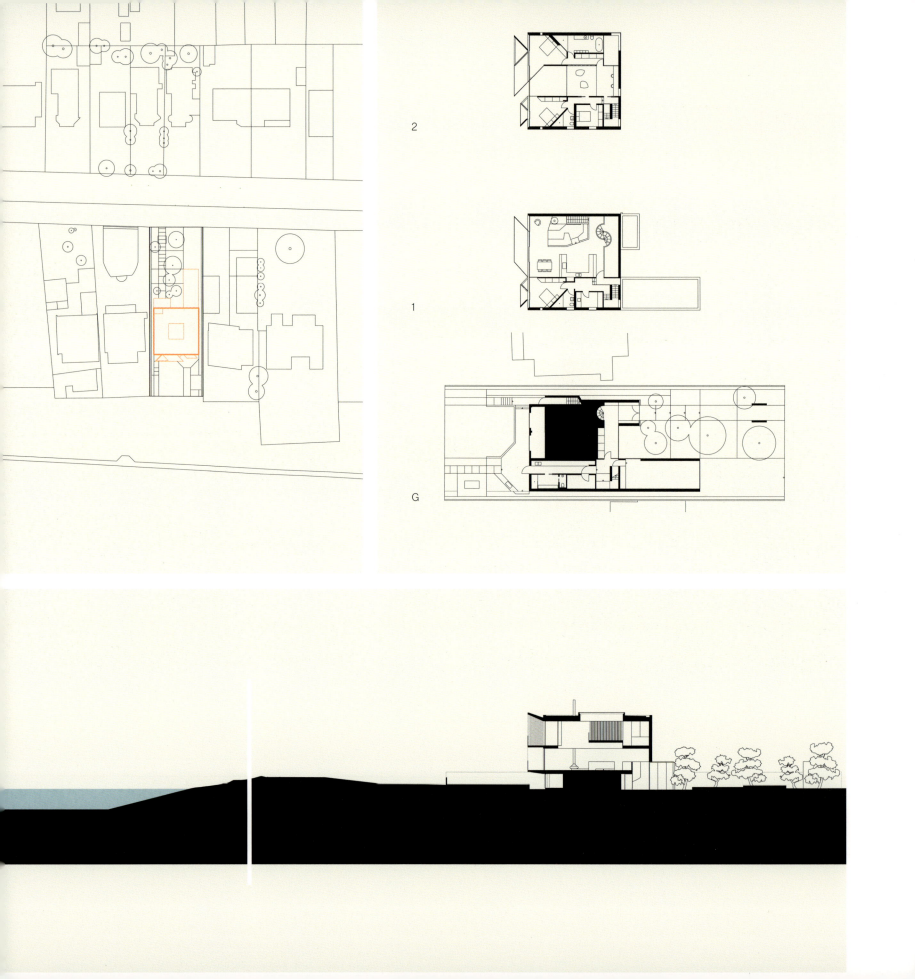

'There is quite a lot going on along Shoreham Beach in terms of replacement buildings, partly because it is quite an exposed location and partly because the quality of the buildings that were put up during the 1950s and 60s was not fantastic', says Gibson. 'So a lot of those earlier buildings have reached the end of their life and need replacing. Our clients bought a post-war house, which was two storeys, with a couple of bedrooms upstairs and dormer windows …'

'The amazing thing about the original house was that there were very few large windows facing the sea,' Nick Eldridge says, 'so the sense of connection with the beach and the water was not good at all. But the great thing for us was that, in terms of the planners, we could more or less do our own thing because there is no architectural consistency on Shoreham Beach.'

For both the practice and its clients, it is undoubtedly a liberating setting in which to work. The neighbouring house is another replacement dwelling and also decidedly contemporary, with a design that places the main living spaces on the upper floor to make the most of the views. It forms part of a disparate sequence of dwellings facing the sea, with a broad spectrum of styles, shapes and roof profiles.

'The planners were very open to ideas', says Gibson. 'As long as you are not going excessively higher than your neighbours, then almost anything goes – particularly if you can demonstrate that you are aiming to deliver something of quality and interest. So the planners were keen to see what we were going to propose to replace the original house.'

Any restrictions and limitations were generated purely by the size and scale of the site itself, including height restrictions as well as the need to protect against potential flood risk and provide a degree of privacy from beach users and walkers making their way along the nearby boardwalk. Eldridge and Gibson decided to raise the three-storey house on a largely solid plinth to protect against the risk of flooding and tidal surge – with the ground floor holding only the entrance as well as ancillary and service spaces, including stores and the plant room. The facade to the access road to the rear is relatively enclosed, but that to the front of the house opens itself up to the water and the coastal vista across the two upper storeys. A triple-height, top-lit entrance hallway naturally entices you upwards via a sculptural feature staircase that ascends to the elevated living area at mid-level.

PAGE 51 View from the beach. Timber screens and reflective glass balustrades provide privacy from the shore.

OPPOSITE Location and floor plans.

OPPOSITE BELOW Cross-section through the elevated living space, sky floor with retractable roof light and double-height entrance.

RIGHT Entrance facade viewed from the road.

**54** UNIQUE HOUSES

'The staircase has been designed as two half-spiral flights, and apart from its shell-like inspiration the geometric form lands at first-floor level facing the open living spaces and the sea', says Eldridge. 'The hallway itself is a three-storey atrium that extends to the top floor, and from the atrium balustrade to the beach facade the living space is open plan with double-height glazing framing sea views.'

Beyond the drama offered by the expansive panorama of the coast, the upper two levels of the house continue to explore dramatic shifts in height and volume. The open-plan living area features a double-height zone at the centre of the floor plan, leading out towards a 'floating' balcony and hosting the dining area with the kitchen alongside. A sunken seating area, with the look and feel of a conversation pit, is arranged to one side, featuring custom sofas facing the open vista but also warmed by a fireplace. This seating zone is lent a degree of intimacy by the way in which it sits under a 'floating', cantilevered box cradling the master bedroom situated on the uppermost storey; the underside of this crafted box is clad in timber, adding warmth and contrasting with the fair-faced concrete floors and plastered walls.

Two additional bedrooms have been positioned towards the other side of the house on the top floor, adding to another guest bedroom at mid-level. Yet another theatrical element at the top of the dwelling is a 'sky room' sitting on a mezzanine gallery 'floating' above the open living area below. The clients had noted the top-floor kitchen in the House in Highgate Cemetery (see page 58), with its retractable skylight that allows the space to open up and become a partially sheltered and fully integrated roof terrace. The sky room at the Shoreham Beach House adopts similar principles.

'The sky room was one of the features of our original concept design responding to the clients' brief for "wow factors" at the outset', says Nick Eldridge. 'There was some discussion about the idea of a sun terrace at the top of the house, but we knew that the planners would resist an actual roof terrace overlooking the beach. So, given that there was a big open volume at the centre of the building, we decided to introduce a mezzanine floor just under the rooflight and that effectively becomes their sun room. Just as in the Highgate Cemetery House, the roof slides back and you can enjoy an open-air platform.'

There is a study area just behind the sky room, which doubles as a bridge that ties the two sides of the top floor together as well as connecting with a secret stairway that serves all three floors of the building. The arrangement of the bedrooms means that the master suite is set somewhat apart from the other three suites, creating a pleasing degree of privacy. A great deal of thought was also given to the way that the beach-facing bedrooms are oriented, with the beds angled so that they pick up on key vistas of the coast; the master bedroom, in particular, is angled in such a way that it looks across the bay towards the east. The integrated, private balconies which complement these bedrooms are framed by angled timber screens that punctuate the fenestration and enrich the facade.

'As well as the master suite, two of the other bedrooms have balconies and their own outdoor space', says Eldridge. 'Together with the open volumes inside the house, this results in a little less floor area but the clients liked the dramatic feel that those double- and triple-height spaces create. Our view is that it is often worth sacrificing some bedroom floor space for additional light and added drama to the living spaces, given that that is where you spend most of your time.'

To achieve such vivid contrasts between open space and more intimate zones, as well as providing elevated and cantilevered elements such as the master bedroom and sky room, clearly required an ambitious level of structural engineering. Steel supports, slimline beams and columns work in close concert with the concrete framework to allow such structural gymnastics.

'There is a sense of surprise when you walk into these spaces', says Gibson. 'When you step in through the rather abstract elevation to the street and into a three-storey void with the sky above you, then that's the first surprise. And then as you go upstairs and into the main living space you see the master bedroom hanging there with no obvious structure supporting it and then you look back and see the sky room. There are a lot of things going on behind the scenes to allow all of this to happen.'

'I think the richness of the internal volumes at Shoreham is really successful', Eldridge says. 'It was a complex three-dimensional design exercise using card models at concept stage followed by computer models and visualisations. Although three years in the making, with construction hijacked by the unexpected, this is a project that upon reflection we all consider well worth the extraordinary efforts made by the team.'

# HOUSE IN HIGHGATE CEMETERY
# HIGHGATE, LONDON

This new house on Highgate's Swains Lane has two distinct faces and personalities. To the street, which dips down towards Dartmouth Park, the dwelling is relatively closed and mysterious, with its sheets of dark granite cladding punctuated by panes of frosted glass. Yet, to the south and west, it opens itself up to the trees and greenery of Highgate Cemetery with banks of floor-to-ceiling glazing and integrated terraces. It is a thoughtful and purposeful juxtaposition that offers the occupants of the house privacy and a sense of connection with the cemetery, which serves as a unique garden offering open vistas and light.

'I was interested in that contrast partly because one of the themes in almost every house I have designed is that the front facade proves enigmatic and obscure but memorable for its scale and material quality', says Nick Eldridge. 'The black granite is designed in such a way that one is unaware of the floor levels behind. It could be an open cube or have four storeys – you just don't know. From the street it becomes an abstract composition but then the rest, apart from the party wall to the north, is entirely in glass.'

The original client for the House in Highgate Cemetery, Richard Elliott, had admired Eldridge Smerin's The Lawns (see pages 98–109), which is nearby and had been shortlisted for the Stirling Prize. Elliott wanted to commission a house that would be as original and successful as The Lawns, if not more so. In this respect, the ambition of the client offered a golden source of encouragement for the practice in producing something exceptional within the Grade I-listed setting.

'The site is just so extraordinary that it demanded a house that was bold', says Elliott. 'I wanted to create the ultimate house here and it was all about the views and the environment. The position of the building alongside the cemetery is by far the most important consideration, and so we wanted to embrace that.'

PAGE 59 View of the house from the south and the tranquil setting of the Grade 1-listed cemetery.

BELOW View from the west of the original steel-framed house designed by John Winter, which had fallen into disrepair. This was one of a group of three terraced houses on the perimeter of the cemetery.

OPPOSITE View from the north-west showing the vertical division of the floor space into one third bedrooms and two thirds living accommodation. The Winter house was divided 50/50 and reflected the lower priority given to kitchen and dining space in the 1960s.

The setting is historic and sensitive in multiple respects. It sits within a Conservation Area while the cemetery itself, dating back to the 1830s, is a listed parkland that is now owned by the Friends of Highgate Cemetery, holding the graves of, among others, Karl Marx, George Eliot, Christina Rossetti, Ralph Richardson, Patrick Caulfield and Richard Elliott's own great-great-grandfather. More than this, the site had been previously occupied by a distinctive steel-framed home designed by the influential English Modernist John Winter. Given that this was an architect whom Nick Eldridge respected – and whose own pioneering, Cor-Ten-clad house sits further along the same street – there were inevitably long discussions about whether it might be possible to update and upgrade the existing building.

'We realised that the existing house had really come to the end of its life', says Eldridge. 'I admired its design but the steel frame had rusted and its cantilevered structure had failed, so it was essentially resting on the cemetery wall. We explored an initial scheme that preserved John Winter's building and extended

it, but it just wasn't viable. We had a meeting with John where I wasn't at all sure about how he would react to the idea of demolishing his house. But he was very understanding, saying that he was fine with it as long as the house that we built in its place was better. After that, I would arrange to meet him from time to time in The Flask [a pub] in Highgate. He taught me about post-war pragmatism and one day showed me around his own home, the Winter House, that had inspired me as a student for its Miesian quality and for the way the glass and steel facades appeared as one surface. He was later very generous in his published review of our project.'

Another issue was a height restriction on the site, which made creating a fresh four-storey house challenging. Richard Elliott managed to overcome the

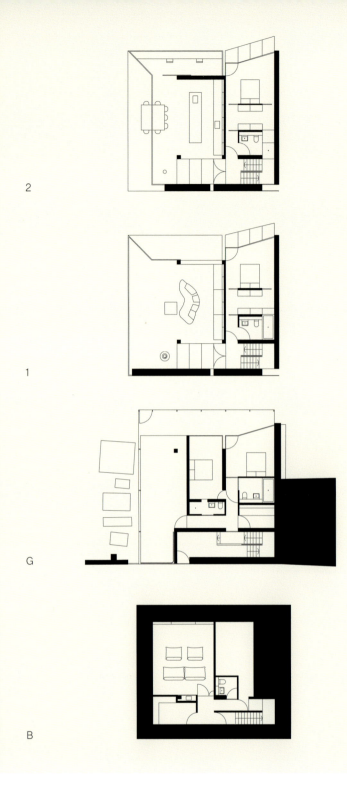

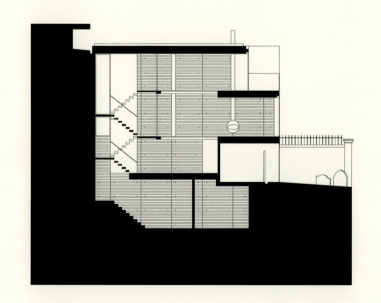

62 UNIQUE HOUSES

OPPOSITE Location and floor plans. The cross section shows the horizontal lines of the board-marked concrete, the spacing of which was determined by the height of the stair treads and generated the vertical dimensions from basement to roof level.

RIGHT The second-floor kitchen and dining space with retractable glass roof, a feature the agents advised the owner not to build but which proved one of the most magical elements of the completed house.

relevant restrictive covenant, which related to the neighbouring building, by buying the house next door and then remodelling and reorienting it. This then allowed Nick Eldridge to push ahead with designing a new house on four levels, including a lower-ground floor hosting a substantial media and music room. The ground floor holds a bedroom and a gym, along with the main entrance lobby and the stairway, where the sunlight filtering down from glass apertures above inevitably draws you upwards towards the main living spaces.

Apart from a separate bedroom suite to one side, much of the first floor is devoted to a spacious living and music room with banks of glass to two sides looking out across the cemetery. An integrated terrace provides an outdoor room here, while enhancing the relationship with the surroundings. Heading up again, there is a similar pattern to the second floor, with a bedroom suite placed against the northern party wall while the rest of the storey is devoted to one of the house's most dramatic spaces: a spacious kitchen, dining area and study with another integrated terrace. At this height, it feels like an escapist retreat floating among the treetops and set apart from the city beyond. The unique character of this part of the house is enriched further by a large skylight that slides open at the touch of a button to create the feeling of a halfway point between inside and outside.

'There were two important aspects of that idea', says Eldridge. 'One was to flood the kitchen with daylight, so on a sunlit day you can just open the whole thing up and it feels very light. But the other consideration was that there is no private garden to the house, if you exclude the cemetery itself, because we built to the edge of the site to maximise space and technically you cannot use the cemetery as a garden, just for walking. So the idea of having a courtyard space at the top of the house, open to the sky, was very attractive, complemented by the open terraces.

'Architecturally, we were able to break down the cube by cutting 2 metre (6½ foot) deep terraces into the first and second floors looking through and over the trees. You also have the greenery of Waterlow Park to the north-east of the cemetery, as well as the cemetery, so the house is totally surrounded by trees. Strangely, the greenery of the trees also seeps beautifully into the house and onto surfaces that reflect their colour. We designed high-gloss, lacquered, black storage units in the living/music room on the first floor, for instance, and so even when you look inwards you still enjoy the reflection of the trees.'

LEFT Glass floors at each level allow light to reach the ground-floor entrance lobby and long views up through the house.

66 UNIQUE HOUSES

OPPOSITE The street facade continues the stepping of the original cemetery wall, introducing steel, etched glass and black granite that echoes the material worked by the monumental masons.

ABOVE The study on the upper level linked to the kitchen and to the master bedroom beyond.

RIGHT The stair viewed from the ground floor entrance lobby. The grain of the timber shuttering for casting the walls transfers to the surface of the concrete and is accentuated by both sunlight and artificial lighting of the space.

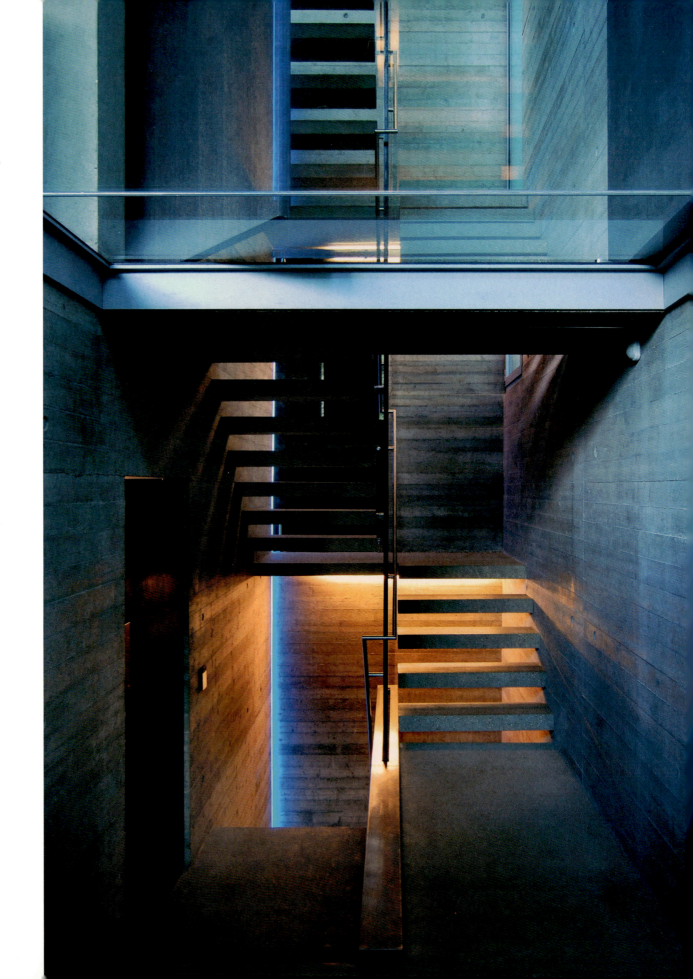

68 UNIQUE HOUSES

Such organic echoes of the surroundings help to soften what is, in many other respects, a decidedly modern interior. In the music room, for example, there are dark stone floors and raw concrete walls and ceilings, which – like the granite on the street elevation – possess a serious degree of monumentality reminiscent of the stone markers and monuments that punctuate the cemetery. Yet the trees beyond the windows are a constant presence, and even the concrete walls offer the imprint and grain of timber – the result of using wooden shuttering against which the concrete was cast. This kind of character is expressed throughout the house, and a similar process happens when it is viewed from the cemetery, as the glass facades mirror the greenery. The dwelling also has a sedum roof, creating a view over a garden of a neighbouring house and further softening the building.

'Although the house does use materials that can be seen as quite cold, it has an interior warmth which is quite unexpected', Eldridge says. 'When the sun is in a certain position casting shadows across the board-marked concrete these walls can look and feel like panels of wood. As an architect, you can never quite anticipate the quality of light, the reflections, the silhouettes, the shadows and the changing nature of a building through the day or through the seasons. So these unexpected views and experiences are always a delight.'

There is certainly a cinematic quality to the house, which has starred in a number of television dramas and photographic shoots. For Richard Elliott, who is a photographer himself, the idea of a photogenic home was part of the initial brief. The new residence certainly met his expectations, as well as receiving RIBA regional and national awards and being shortlisted in 2009 for the London Building of the Year, the Manser Medal and the Stephen Lawrence Prize.

'There were a few objections from neighbours right at the beginning, but everyone who objected came forward later and told me that they rather liked the house', says Elliott, who has since moved on.

With this in mind, it seems only correct to refer back to John Winter, who wrote an article about the house for *Architecture Today* (July/August 2008). Winter was gracious and generous, recognising the rare beauty of the site itself but also offering praise for the design: 'I am lost in admiration for the excellence of the building work and the thorough rigour of the design', wrote Winter, who died in 2012. 'This comes as near to being a faultless building as I have seen for a long time.'

# COR-TEN HOUSE
# PUTNEY, LONDON

For a practice with a particular interest in the intrinsic character of materials – together with their texture, patina and provenance – Cor-Ten is a subject of fascination. It is a kind of steel in which the exterior surface of the metal is purposefully encouraged to rust so that it forms a protective layer on the outer surface of a building. At the same time, the earthy patina that results from this gentle rusting process suggests both the industrial and the organic, with colour tones that look decidedly natural even though the material is factory-made.

This kind of weathered steel was first developed in the 1930s and initially used to make hopper cars and containers for use on American railroads. Cor-Ten only attracted the attention of architects, designers and sculptors after the Finnish-American modernist master Eero Saarinen used the steel for his John Deere Headquarters in Moline, Illinois (1964). For a manufacturer of agricultural machinery, this combination of the industrial and the earthily organic seemed apposite, with the use of Cor-Ten first suggested by the company's president.

Over time, the material has been increasingly used in the United States for contemporary residential buildings. In the UK, however, it is still unusual. One of the earliest uses in a domestic context was the innovative house that John Winter designed for himself in Swains Lane, Highgate, in 1969, which was later listed by English Heritage. Nick Eldridge was given a tour of this house by the architect, whose work he admired, around the time that the practice was working on its own residential project further up the same street (see pages 58–69). Later, when Eldridge London was working on the design of a new house in Putney, the use of Cor-Ten became a key part of this fresh and original suburban home.

'The intention behind the whole house was that it should be like a piece of sculpture', says Eldridge. 'The facade is really this seamlessly welded sheet

PAGE 71 The street facade reinterprets the traditional English bay window and dormer using only two materials, glass and Cor-Ten steel, which weathers to the colours of the neighbouring brick walls and tile roofs.

BELOW Concept cross-section.

OPPOSITE Plans. Street Elevation showing the new house in context.

of oxidising Cor-Ten steel, prefabricated off-site by skilled welders in Suffolk. It is the kind of construction technology you could use to make a ship's hull, so it should certainly be watertight. It is a brilliant system, actually – both watertight and structural at the same time.

Eldridge's clients have a long relationship with the site itself. One of them grew up in the neighbouring red-brick house until his father decided to partition off the garden, sell the period building and construct a new family home alongside it. Many years later, the couple inherited this house but agreed that the design was flawed and, given that they share an interest in architecture and design, that they would love to build a new and bespoke house on the site. A chance meeting with Nick Eldridge eventually led to the first conversations about a commission.

'He is an antiques dealer and an expert consultant to museums', Eldridge says. 'As a one-time collector of cutlery, I discovered a stall inside one of the galleries on the Portobello Road one Saturday morning and began talking to the couple who owned it about a harlequin set of Georgian three-pronged forks they had bundled up on a table. They were too expensive for me, but we exchanged cards. Two weeks later I received a call asking if I would be interested in designing a house for them.'

The clients came with many ideas and points of reference in mind, which fed into initial discussions about the project. These included an admiration for Japanese design and interiors, a love of the Arts and Crafts architecture and

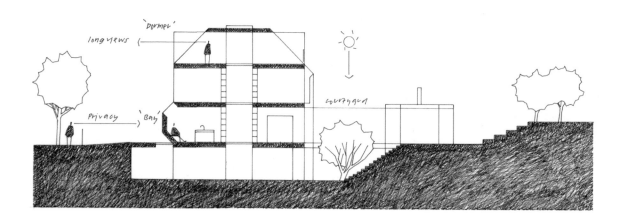

72 UNIQUE HOUSES

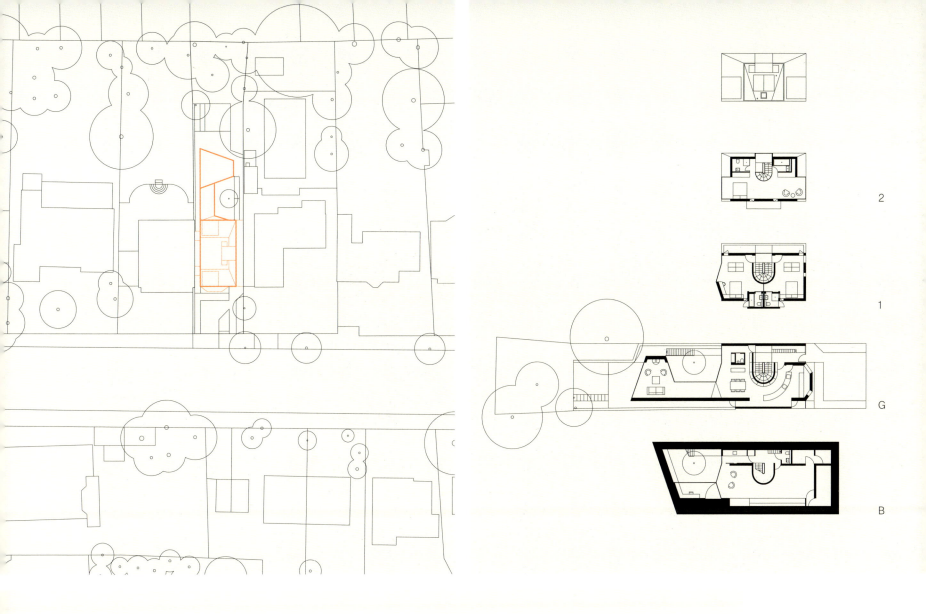

LEFT View from the courtyard shortly after completion and before the flowering of the Amelanchier. The building was designed to allow daylight and sunlight to all parts of the house while maintaining privacy.

design of Greene & Greene and an affection, in particular, for the work of Marcel Breuer. Such influences offered an eclectic mixture in terms of inspiration, yet also pointed to an intelligent understanding of architectural design and the wish to create something different and original when it came to their own home.

'The clients told us about how much they liked Breuer and Greene & Greene', says Eldridge. 'So I racked my brains to think about how we might turn those references into something that would inform this building. I had lived in New York for a while, so I thought back to my experiences of the Whitney Museum of American Art [completed by Breuer in 1966] and remembered a famous photograph of Breuer, taken when the museum opened, against a little window that projects out onto the street frontage. So I was thinking about that projecting window and also how that might connect with bay windows in the traditional London vernacular. The idea of a modern version of a projecting bay, and also the colour of the Cor-Ten being a similar colour to the brick and tiles of the neighbouring houses, worked in our favour with the planners and the local conservation officers ...'

The distinctive Cor-Ten facade features a projecting bay window at ground-floor level that resembles a camera lens or viewfinder, but with a central sheet of oxidised steel where you might expect to find a plate of glass. To the top and sides, this Cor-Ten plate is bordered by angled glazing panels while the fourth angled plate at the bottom of the bay is also in Cor-Ten, forming a window seat inside the house, in the kitchen. This composition seems somewhat abstract until you begin to understand the geometry of this bay window, or projecting lens, as well as its relationship to the front door alongside; the two vertical slot windows at first-floor level; and the raised dormer at the top of the building, reminiscent of Breuer's Whitney apertures.

'Part of the idea of the design of the bay was to create a degree of privacy for the kitchen at the front, but still allow it to function as a window', says Eldridge. 'When someone comes up to the front door, you can look through the glass side panel and see who it is. So the front elevation is enigmatic and sculptural at the same time, complemented by this contrast in materials between the Cor-Ten and the glass. While such glass technology was not available to John Winter in the 1960s, we were able to use stepped-edge double-glazed units to achieve a flush detail between glass and Cor-Ten steel without frames, which added to the sculptural precision of this house as an object free of any recognisable vernacular.'

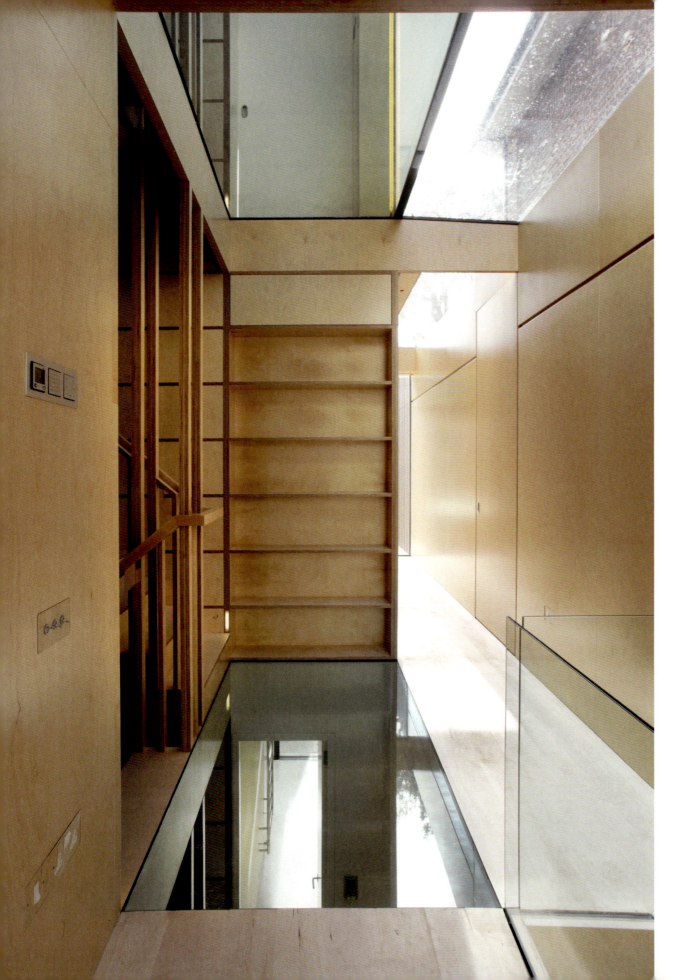

LEFT Viewed from the entrance, the principal staircase is to the left, the stair dedicated to the dogs is to the right.

OPPOSITE A feature of the house is the interesting juxtaposition of the architect's simply detailed raw materials and the clients' collection of art and furniture of different periods which makes it a home of great personality and charm.

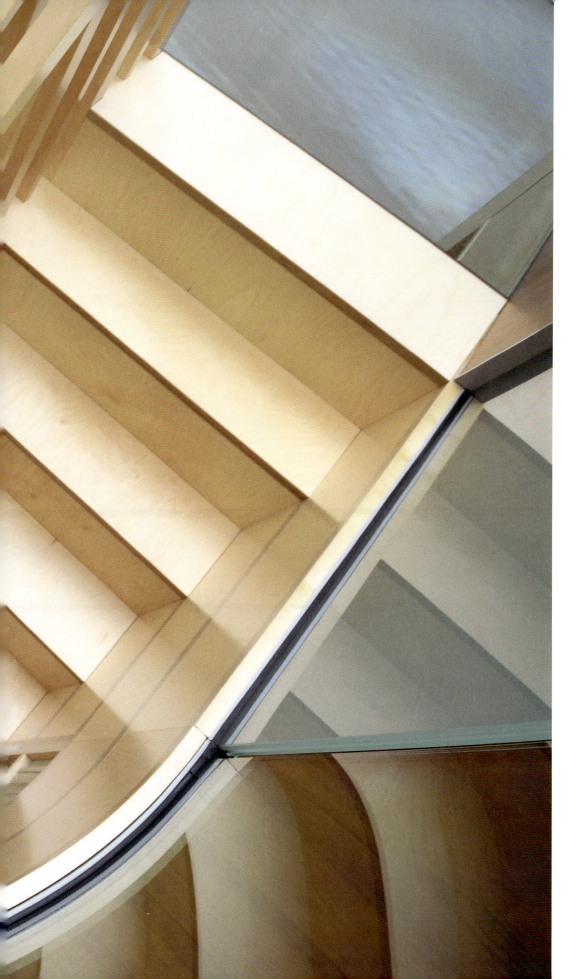

LEFT Looking down from the master bedroom with its Japanese tatami mat flooring, the birch plywood staircase is lined with books down to the ground floor.

RIGHT  View to the sky from
the ground-floor entrance.

**80**  UNIQUE HOUSES

Stepping inside, the floor plan revolves around the need to make the most of a narrow site and to maximise available space, as well as providing privacy from the neighbouring houses and amplifying both the available light and key connections to outdoor living spaces. The solutions to these complex problems are multiple, partly involving the creation of a sunken courtyard at lower-ground level (holding a lounge and study) and a single-storey glass-and-timber outrigger at ground-floor level, which pushes out into the back garden while hosting the main living space arranged around an integrated fireplace.

'It is unusual to be allowed to extend further into the garden,' says Eldridge, 'but the concept of creating a planted courtyard between the rear wall of the house and living space beyond was supported by the conservation and design officer, who understood the rationale for letting light into all parts of the garden-level living space as well as the study below.'

The connecting feature between all four levels of the house is the horseshoe-shaped staircase, which also serves – at key points – as a library, bordered by bookshelves. The staircase carries on upwards towards the two guest bedrooms on the first floor and the spacious master suite on the top level. The crafted quality of such elements ties in well with the Arts and Crafts references, while the proportions of the bedroom on the second floor were designed around the dimensions of the *tatami* mat seen in Japanese homes. In this way, each point of inspiration mentioned by the clients was met.

The principal staircase is actually one of three stairways in the house. Along with a secondary staircase leading from the sunken courtyard to the back garden, there is a dedicated dog stair by the front door that takes the pets directly down to the basement level, where they – and their owners – can access the utility room.

Returning to the Cor-Ten, it manages the almost impossible task of tying in with the colour tones of the streetscape while also helping to create something dynamic and original within it: 'We undertook a good deal of research into the material and the form', says Eldridge. 'If the vertical surfaces get wet that's absolutely fine, but you should not use it for horizontal planes. At different times of day and in different light conditions, it becomes an ever-changing surface – and when the sun comes out, the steel turns a brilliant orange. It is a beautiful material, and this is one of my favourite street facades.'

# GARDEN HOUSE
# HIGHGATE, LONDON

The Garden House forms part of an unusual twin commission for not just one but two new, bespoke houses. Eldridge London's clients initially approached the practice to discuss the design and build of a home by the sea in Shoreham, West Sussex (see pages 50–57). But then the client – an entrepreneur in the tech industry – and his partner acquired a site in London and asked Nick Eldridge and Mike Gibson if they would also design a family home in this very different urban context.

'The clients were living on the other side of Waterlow Park from our House in Highgate Cemetery, on Swains Lane (see pages 58–69), so they were aware of that house and of our work', says Mike Gibson. 'They had seen the sliding skylight at Swains Lane and other elements of the design, and wanted an architect who could deliver these kind of things for them. They didn't have a fully formed brief, but one thing that they were very definite about was that they wanted a "wow factor". Of the two projects, it became a priority to get the London house ready first, so the Garden House jumped the queue in front of Shoreham.'

The spacious site consisted of the former garden and garages to a Victorian mansion block, sitting within a neighbourhood that is also rich in parkland and green spaces. Acquired with outline planning permission for a new residence already in place, the parcel of land sits to the rear of the mansion block, accessed by a private driveway – with privacy enhanced by the sloping gradient of the site as it steps down to the garden, as well as a borderland of mature trees that helps to protect and soften the setting.

'The developer of the Victorian block, which was updated about five years ago, obtained planning permission for a residence on the garden site', Gibson says. 'But it was rather oddly planned, so after our clients bought the land it became

PAGE 83 Bedrooms suspended over the double-height living space create changing views to the landscape. The bridge-like structure allows the entire length of the glazing to slide open to the terrace and garden.

PAGES 84–85 The south-facing facade looks out over a terrace and garden designed for entertaining in the secluded neighbourhood of leafy Highgate Village.

OPPOSITE Floor plans. Cross section through the double-height living space, open courtyard and spa pool.

our job to create a house here that they would be happy living in and which would have the level of design ambition they were looking for. The site itself is quite long, so even with the new house the garden that was retained is substantial.'

'In some respects there are certain similarities with Greenways, in Coombe Park (see pages 20–37), at least in terms of the site', says Nick Eldridge. 'In both cases, as you arrive, it is a sloping site where it makes sense to enter the building on an upper level and then step down into the main living space and towards the rear garden. So with both houses you also have this processional entrance and a journey down a sculptural staircase before reaching the heart of the house when the open views reveal themselves. But with the Garden House you are also stepping into double-height volumes of the main living spaces, so that offers added drama.'

The new building has been thoughtfully oriented so that it fully connects with the garden while offering a vivid indoor–outdoor relationship. The main approach, then, is at upper-ground level, where a garage and guest bedroom sit to the rear of the plan while three principal bedrooms – including the master suite – push outwards towards the garden. Each of these elevated bedrooms features floor-to-ceiling plates of glass framing glimpses of the cityscape beyond the treeline, with integrated Juliet balconies allowing these spaces to unfold in the warmer months. The projecting volume holding the master suite has a slightly higher roofline, allowing for an additional mezzanine level with a 'floating' en-suite bathroom at the highest point in the house.

The entrance hall on the upper storey connects with a line of circulation that offers glimpses over the two double-height voids, or atria, that sit between the three projecting, linear units holding the triptych of principal bedrooms. From this landing, one can both look down to the open living spaces on the floor below and also across the atria and through banks of glass to the garden.

The hallway leads directly towards a spiral stairway that sits right at the heart of the plan. Made with a concrete helix and plywood sides and balustrades, the entire piece has been coated in resin to create a smooth and uniform finish and then spray-painted a vivid crimson. As such, the staircase becomes a theatrical focal point like a vertical red carpet, while the choice of colour means that it becomes a beacon naturally guiding guests and visitors downstairs to the communal and most social part of the home.

**86** UNIQUE HOUSES

1

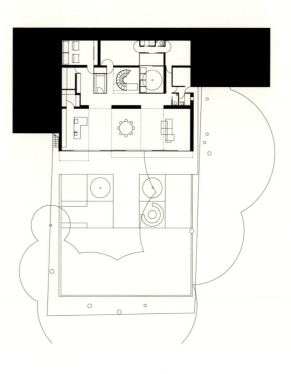

G

B

LEFT The helical stair links the entrance at the upper level with the living space at garden level.

OPPOSITE The wine room stands between the kitchen and the entertainment spaces cut into the ground at the rear of the building.

LEFT From the entrance with its marble floor is a view of the canopy of an ancient olive tree within an open courtyard bringing light into the heart of the building.

BELOW The organic form of the helical stair contrasts with the muted surfaces of the concrete walls and geometric parquet floors.

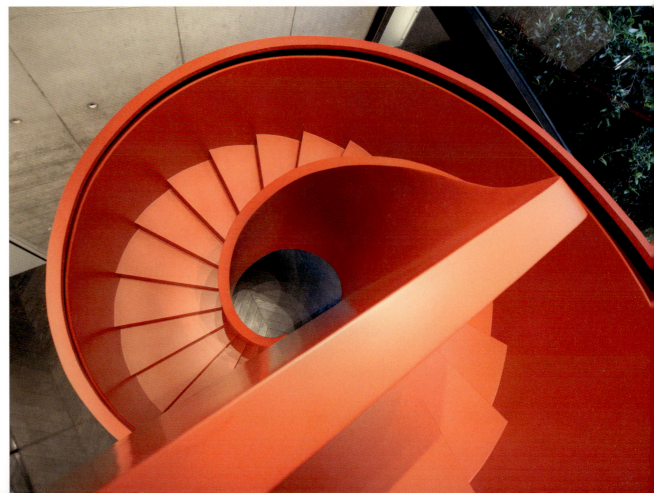

'The red staircase was actually included in the first renders that we showed to the clients, during a quasi-competition stage right at the beginning of the process', says Gibson. 'We were really putting our best foot forward and so we went with this bold statement staircase at the heart of the building. Though its shape evolved, they loved this red staircase from the start. But also the planning of most of the building is quite linear and rigorous, with some dark colours for the materials, so we wanted something vibrant that would introduce life and personality.'

Additional drama comes from a sunken and glass-walled courtyard sitting alongside the staircase and occupied by a mature olive tree. The courtyard offers an opportunity to bring the garden directly into the home itself as well as doubling as a lightwell, while the tree is like an extraordinary organic installation adding another layer of character with a natural focal point that contrasts with the sculptural stairway.

'The husband is English but his wife is South American, so there was also this idea of a co-relationship between some very English planting and landscaping in the garden along with elements from a warmer climate', Gibson says. 'So the olive tree does have this special resonance for them and obviously the trunk of this ancient tree, which they imported from Barcelona, has this amazing age and personality to it. The tree has its own little microclimate in that courtyard, which is warmer than an open garden, so it seems to quite enjoy being in there. But it's also this wonderful secret that only reveals itself when you are actually inside the house.'

Downstairs, on the lower-ground level, the side-by-side staircase and courtyard remain the lynchpins of the floor plan. Towards the more enclosed rear section of the house, where the lower-ground floor embeds itself into the slope of the land, the practice designed a run of low-light leisure spaces including a home cinema, a club/music room and a gym/playroom, while a home spa pool borrows sunlight from the sunken courtyard. Other amenity spaces on the lower-ground floor include a wine store, storage rooms and a pantry/back kitchen.

The rest of the ground floor is devoted to a generously scaled and open-plan living area, looking out on and connecting with the landscaped garden. The double-height voids add to the sense of openness and enhance the quality of light here, while the entire space is unified by a rounded palette of materials – including herringbone oak floors with a dark finish and tulip-wood ceilings spray-finished in a similar charcoal tone to the floors.

92 UNIQUE HOUSES

OPPOSITE The living space with a glimpse of the open courtyard beyond.

RIGHT View from the spa pool to the open courtyard planted with a 200-year-old olive tree.

Encompassing a seating area at one end, a dining area at the centre and a custom kitchen at the opposite end, the entire space opens up to the adjoining terrace and garden via a sliding wall of floor-to-ceiling glass. Once retracted, the line between inside and outside space dissolves and fades away – while for the family, the garden and greenery become part of the house itself.

'We have a sequence of square planters and new landscaping with the mature trees beyond, positioned around the edge of the garden', says Gibson. 'One of the things that the clients really liked was the seclusion that the design gives you, because when you get to the house you are already away from the neighbours and by the time you come down to the living area you are in this protected enclave or secret garden. They wanted the house to feel integrated with the garden, so we designed the landscaping to make sure that they coordinate with one another and then the garden becomes another room that the family can use. This idea of an indoor–outdoor lifestyle was very much part of the brief from the start.'

While the aforementioned Greenways project also encompassed a level of bespoke detailing that carried through to the furniture and furnishings, the interiors here have been designed to be flexible enough to accommodate the owners' own choices of furniture and art – offering the opportunity to layer these spaces according to their own personalities. Another consideration, given that the Garden House is one of two consecutive projects for the same clients, was that each dwelling should be very different from the other.

'Both projects have a cleanness and crispness to the architecture', Gibson says. 'But they wanted a very different character to each of them. The London house has these dark materials and polished finishes, while the beach house is intended to be much lighter and more natural.'

'The clients enjoy travelling and picking up ideas from hotels or places they have stayed', says Eldridge. 'So they have ideas of their own about the interiors – and part of the fun of these two houses is that they have been able to express themselves. Clients don't always want to feel that the architect is designing everything in the house. They want the interiors to reflect who they are, so it is about creating spaces that allow them to shape their surroundings. At the end of the day, it is their family home and we would like to think the architecture is strong enough to accommodate whatever they choose to furnish the house.'

OPPOSITE View from the garden at night.

# RENEW

Adaptive and inventive repurposing of existing buildings has always been an important part of Nick Eldridge's work. While many assume that The Stirling Prize shortlisted Highgate house, known as The Lawns, which won the architect's young practice such attention and acclaim, was a new building, the truth was that it was a thoughtful reinvention of an existing house.

Ever since the success of The Lawns, Nick Eldridge has welcomed the idea of giving fresh relevance to period buildings through such imaginative adaptation. The practice's interventions and extensions have often been radical and transformative, aimed at creating a 'modern' home suited to contemporary lifestyles and patterns of living. At times, such new additions have become the fresh focal point of the home, as seen in the House in Belsize Park, for example, where the new 'extension' is now the hub of family life.

As questions of sustainability and concerns about embedded energy lead, increasingly, to the repurposing of existing buildings rather then replacement, such reinventions offer key exemplars of greener solutions. More recently, Eldridge has reworked a characterful period barn in Cornwall not only to provide a new home and studio for himself and his family, but as a way of exploring fresh ideas related to the thoughtful renewal of valuable buildings that are also rich in history, materiality and craftsmanship.

# THE LAWNS, HIGHGATE
# LONDON

While Highgate and Hampstead might be dominated by picturesque rows of Georgian and Victorian houses, there is also a 'tradition' of modernist-inspired architectural experimentation here that stretches back to the 1930s. This was the era of Ernö Goldfinger's collection of three houses on Willow Road (1939) alongside Hampstead Heath – including the architect's own home, which is now in the hands of the National Trust. There was also Connell, Ward and Lucas's 66 Frognal (1938), Tayler & Green's house for artist Roger Pettiward (1938) and Wells Coates' Isokon building in Belsize Park (1934). Later, during the 1960s and 70s, another wave of innovative buildings punctuated this part of North London, including houses by architects Michael and Patty Hopkins; John Winter (see page 60); and Leonard Manasseh, who built three houses in Highgate including one for himself and another known as The Lawns.

Manasseh was best known for designing the home of the National Motor Museum for Lord Montagu at Beaulieu (1964) as well as his work for the Festival of Britain, which first established his reputation. The Lawns was built during the 1950s on the site of a Victorian house, which retained a presence there in the form of a substantial basement level. The house eventually caught the attention of husband and wife designers John and Frances Sorrell, who were taken not so much by the architecture but by the extraordinary hilltop location looking out over Highgate and Hampstead towards the cityscape beyond. It was, in part, the desire to make the most of this vista that led the Sorrells to Nick Eldridge and Piers Smerin and a commission to reinvent The Lawns in a way that would connect the house with its surroundings and offer the family a house tailored to their own needs and preferences.

PAGE 99 The house viewed from Pond Square and flanked by the traditional Georgian and Victorian houses of the Highgate Conservation area.

RIGHT The Lawns in 1998. In the 1980s the flat-roofed modernist house designed by Leonard Manasseh had acquired a pitched roof and other extensions, detracting from the quality of the 1950s design.

'The Sorrells had just sold their design-and-identity practice to Interbrand and were beginning to step back from it, but John was also Chairman of the Design Council at the time, where my wife was working, helping with the move into their new headquarters', says Eldridge. 'So we were introduced to them just at the point where they had some time and the opportunity to create a new home for themselves and were looking for some guidance as to whether they should demolish the Manasseh house and start again or if they should work with it. Apparently, every other architect that the Sorrells interviewed for the project was going to sweep it away – but we never entertained that idea. I always felt instinctively that something would be lost if the Manasseh house completely disappeared.'

Having decided to launch their own practice, The Lawns became Eldridge Smerin's first commission. In many respects, the Sorrells were the perfect clients

**100** UNIQUE HOUSES

given that – as designers themselves – they were very well informed, as well as clear about the way that they and their two children wanted to live. Yet, at the same time, they were also acutely aware of the need to allow their chosen architects the freedom to express and progress their ideas, taking a highly receptive approach to their suggestions.

From a planning point of view, the architects and their clients were helped by a number of factors. The Manasseh house was not listed and sat on a site with its own precedent of adaptation, evolution and change, including additional alterations made during the 1980s. Perhaps more importantly, the two-storey dwelling was topped by a tall, pitched roof that could be replaced with an additional floor level that would make the most of the key vistas out across the city.

'Combined with the location itself, the pitched roof, which had been added later to Leonard's flat roof, was useful and made it possible for us to transform the existing house from an inward-looking building into something much more extraordinary', says Eldridge. 'But that also involved searching for the legibility of Manasseh's building. When I imagined removing the roof and taking away additions to the front and sides, actually what was left was this very pure box at the centre with an interesting history attached. The front facade was not that promising but the frame of the rear elevation had a rigorous geometry to it that was almost Louis Kahn-like. We imagined rendering some of the brickwork and simplifying the windows with larger panels of glass and a vertically proportioned opening light in each bay. With all the later additions stripped away, there was the possibility of using the space to the front and the sides of Leonard's structure and adding rooms that were, by contrast with this and the neighbouring houses in the Conservation Area, very contemporary.'

In this way, Eldridge Smerin began designing what is effectively a new building around the core of the old. The existing basement level was retained for use by the Sorrell's children while the old house was stripped back and retained, with its rigorous rectangular grid offering a kind of anchor for the reinvented house. A double-height entrance atrium was added at the front, creating a fresh facade with a strong geometrical character of its own, while the architects introduced a new principal staircase within this space, which also doubled as a gallery for displaying works by the painter Terry Frost.

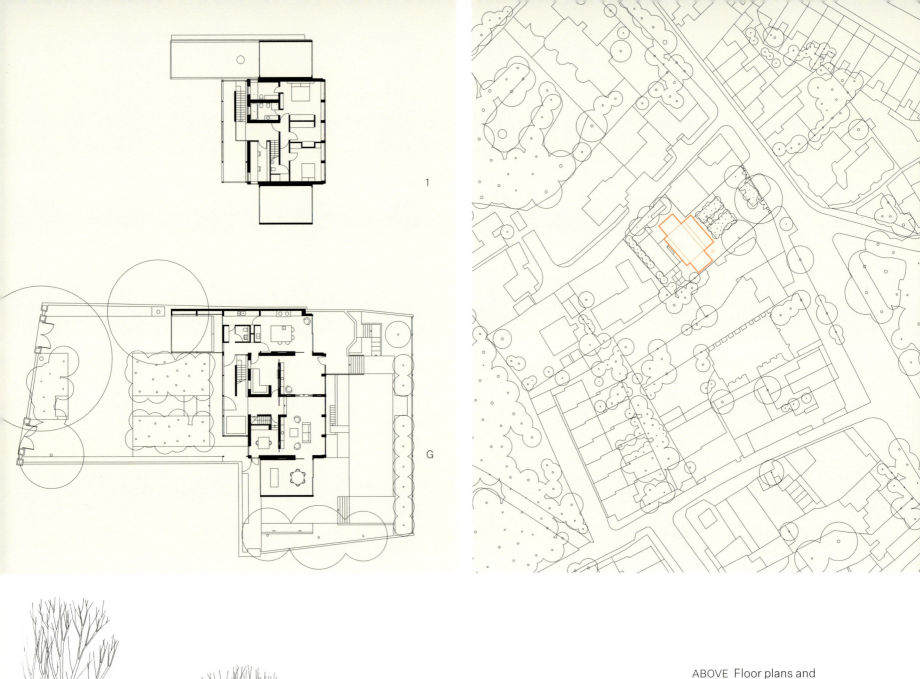

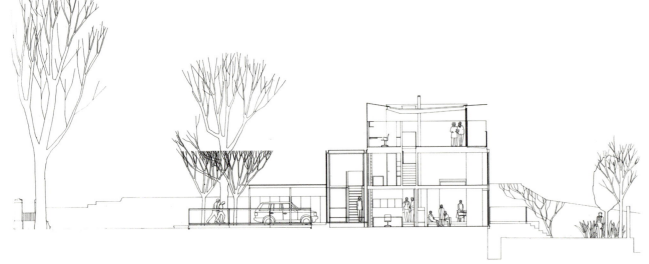

ABOVE Floor plans and location plan.

LEFT Hand-drawn animated cross section by Nick Eldridge, drawn for John and Frances Sorrell. Although it was Nick's hope that the new trees at the front of the house would be clipped each year to the height of the entrance porch, they grew taller.

PAGE 103 View from the front entrance path when the silver birches were newly planted. The top floor studio was designed to merge with the sky.

LEFT The white studio space looking south to the terrace with panoramic views across London.

BELOW The visual lightness of the top floor is achieved through a carefully detailed structural glass wall and roof with minimal interruption of its transparency.

To one side of the building, the practice created a spacious, steel-framed, new double-height kitchen, leading out through 4 metre (13 foot) high sliding glass doors to a terrace overlooking the rear garden, which was landscaped by Dan Pearson. To the other side, there is now a conservatory, equal in size to the kitchen structure, which also connects through to a terrace but which features a solid side wall that offers privacy from the neighbouring house. The old house was partially opened up to these new additions, with fluid connections to a dining area and living room that offer a much stronger relationship than hitherto with the back garden via the revised and enriched fenestration. Two smaller rooms at the centre of the plan became a study for Frances Sorrell and a media room.

'The idea was that those smaller spaces in the existing house would become the inner sanctum', says Eldridge. 'But the larger, shared spaces would connect with the garden and the new extensions. We designed those spaces in such a way that you can slide doors across to open them up or shut them down. This idea of being able to open and close space was repeated on the first floor with a pivoting door, which allowed a view of trees and sky from the bedroom corridor when open, and when closed linked the bedroom to an en-suite bathroom tucked into the space beneath the staircase to the newly created second floor. The structure and window openings of the existing building were retained as a palimpsest, in which, without expressing any of the original materials, the white-painted walls and panels of white glass in the openings are reminders of the old house.'

One of the most dramatic and photogenic spaces in the house was the new studio added at the top of the house in place of the old, pitched roof. This is a glass-sided box, which some have described as Miesian, 'floating' on top of the original core building. Largely open plan and beautifully detailed, the studio splices the feeling of an enticing penthouse with the quality of a belvedere, offering – at last – those open panoramas right across the bowl of central London. The Sorrells described this studio – where the walls, ceilings and almost all pieces of furniture were white – as 'our thinking space'.

'The principal idea was to use as much glass as possible so that the top floor would almost dematerialise and simply reflect the sky and the trees', Eldridge says. 'That was accepted by the planners, who acknowledged the visual lightness and elegance of the new proposal. Given that all the living spaces are on the lower floors and in the core of the old house, it did enable that top floor to be relatively unencumbered and open plan.'

Importantly for the practice, the Sorrells' level of ambition was carried through into every aspect of the interiors and gardens. The couple's art collection needed to be thoughtfully accommodated, for instance, and the level of detailing and finishing was to be of the highest standard. The Lawns had to serve the needs of the family but also open itself up when the Sorrells were entertaining.

'If you do your house really well, people tend to think it is self-indulgent', John Sorrell has said in the past. 'That is complete nonsense: what could be more important than the environment you live in? I am amazed people are prepared to put up with environments that don't work and which drive them crazy every day of their lives.'

'They were very wary about being prescriptive but they also allowed me to design a lot of built-in and loose furniture for the house, which I found really rewarding', says Eldridge. 'Sometimes a client will just move into the house with things they already have or pieces that are slightly alien to the new space. But with the Sorrells it was completely different. Everything that they brought into the house added up and it was, in the end, incredibly cohesive. Frances's study, for instance, was carefully designed with a Bill Amberg leather floor. Here I designed a very pure, square desk for her in oak with an Amberg leather top matching the floor and then oak storage. It was a joy to design those pieces and to work with the craftspeople who made them.'

Such involvement in both architecture and interiors, as well as furniture and furnishings, was important for the evolution of the practice and its future work. Just as important was an RIBA Award and a shortlisting for the Stirling Prize – with The Lawns becoming the very first residential project to make it onto the Stirling list, which was won in 2001 by WilkinsonEyre's Magna Centre in Rotherham. It was, by any standards, an amazing achievement for a new practice, with the RIBA judges noting this 'exemplary example of how the 21st Century house can be incorporated into historic conservation areas as part of the continuing evolution of domestic architecture'.

'The house was beautiful to live in', says Frances Sorrell, looking back at the project now. 'What transformed the house were the two extensions that replaced

BELOW To the left of the stair is one of the original window openings of the front facade of the 1950s house. At the far end of the entrance hall and above a black water feature is hung *Through Blues* by Terry Frost.

RIGHT The glazed west extension with low window looking onto gently cascading water spouts was designed for privacy from houses beyond. On the screen wall is hung a chalk cliff relief by the Boyle family.

the existing garage and conservatory and gave us these two large, high-ceilinged rooms overlooking the garden – as well as the studio, which gave us wonderful views over London to the rear and Pond Square to the front. Having a choice of different spaces was wonderful too. At the time we moved in our sons were teenagers, so having their own accommodation in the basement worked really well for us all. We enjoyed looking at it, living in it and sharing it. The house changed how we lived.'

The decision not to demolish Manasseh's house but to reinvent it now seems enlightened. It fits with the growing demand for the adaptive reuse of existing buildings, making the most of their embedded energy and inbuilt carbon footprint with sustainability in mind. It was also a mark of respect for Manasseh's own contribution to The Lawns, with the architect continuing to live in Highgate until he passed away in 2017.

'Given our own lack of experience at the time, getting planning permission for The Lawns in a Conservation Area was quite an achievement that may have benefitted from our own naivety', Eldridge says. 'We were young and brave with our ideas. We did not want to upset Leonard Manasseh but chose to retain the core of his house on its own merit. When we met to discuss the project, he was complimentary and pragmatic: "Life goes on," he said, "just do it well". The Sorrells used to invite him to the house quite regularly. At their Christmas parties, he would sit by the fireplace in the living room with a black notebook and write everything down because he said that he had a terrible memory. It would be wonderful to read those notebooks now.'

OPPOSITE View from the garden at night showing the simplification and remodelling of the 1950s core of the Manasseh house and extended wings and rooftop studio.

# HOUSE IN BELSIZE PARK LONDON

There are times when the impetus to enlarge or extend an existing building can become a radically transformative process. This project in Belsize Park, North London, for example, could simply be described as an extension to an existing period building. Yet the addition of a new, glass-sided pavilion has created an entirely fresh focal point for this family home, hosting open-plan living spaces arranged around a secret garden. In doing so, a redundant and semi-derelict Victorian coach house and folly were also given a new lease of life, becoming part of an imaginative and original 21st-century home.

'The glass pavilion really provides the living spaces and the fun spaces for the family,' says Nick Eldridge, 'as well as offering a source of daylight and sunlight. It has become a very important part of the house and it does seem like quite a dominant element as you come through the garden gate and discover that there is more of the house than you might have been expecting. But from the street outside, the extension is actually very low key and the planners were very keen that you couldn't really see this new element hidden behind the boundary wall. So it is both transformative and discreet.'

The clients for the project were Charles and Seema Perez, who had been living in Belsize Park for some years and, with three children, were outgrowing their maisonette apartment. They could see, from their former home, an empty red-brick house with an overgrown garden, and became increasingly fascinated by it.

'We were struck by the idea of having this forgotten piece of land in the middle of NW3 that had all this potential,' says Seema Perez. 'From our maisonette we could see this overgrown, wild site that was being used as a dumping ground and every now and then people would come along and throw things over the wall. But then, one day, a "for sale" went up and I phoned Charles at work.

PAGE 111 The glazed open-plan family space merges with the landscape. Perched at the upper level is the study looking out over the planted roof and towards the extended Victorian house and church beyond.

OPPOSITE The triangular motif of canopy and roof-light is generated by the geometry of the site.

RIGHT The open-plan pavilion provides a flexible living space with kitchen, dining and sitting areas linked to the main house and courtyard.

OPPOSITE Floor plans and cross section through the main house, courtyard and glazed pavilion.

We both went to see it and decided, in the end, that we would like to try and do something with it.'

The site was unusual in many respects. The coach store, and the modest home alongside it, had been built for his coachman by the former Mayor of Hampstead, Henry Harben, who lived just around the corner. The meeting of two neighbouring roads created a triangular parcel of land alongside the house that had once been home to a kitchen garden and glasshouses, which had long since disappeared. Earlier plans for the site, which had included the idea of knocking down the Victorian buildings, had been vetoed by the local planners and conservation officers. But Seema and Charles Perez were keen to keep the existing elements and work imaginatively and sensitively around them.

During the press coverage of the 2001 Stirling Prize, the couple had noted The Lawns (see pages 98–109) – another project that had involved the reinvention and transformation of an existing building. They contacted Nick Eldridge and his former colleague Piers Smerin, asking their practice to work on ideas for the site that made the most of its garden setting.

'Our brief to Nick and Piers included a courtyard, because we have always loved courtyard spaces', says Seema Perez. 'We liked the idea of a small, unassuming doorway that gives way to the unexpected – and the entrance to the courtyard garden is very much like that. The garden is an amazing part of the project and really the first "room" that you come into. Because it was quite overgrown when we bought the site, we decided that we wanted a woodland feel to it that would soften the modern building. Jinny Blom designed the garden for us with silver birch trees and lots of wild flowers. It's like wandering into a secluded glade.'

The new and largely single-storey addition pushes out into this secret garden, with glass walls allowing the greenery to become a constant presence that can be enjoyed from inside as well as outside. The design of the new building also gives the family the courtyard space that they had hoped for, wrapping its way around a partially sheltered outdoor room. Inside, the pavilion is flexible and open, allowing the family to shape and zone their living space as they wish. A custom kitchen has been pushed to the rear, liberating the rest of this generously proportioned room, while the use of sliding glass walls and concrete floors both inside and outside allows the boundary between the pavilion and the courtyard to dissolve in

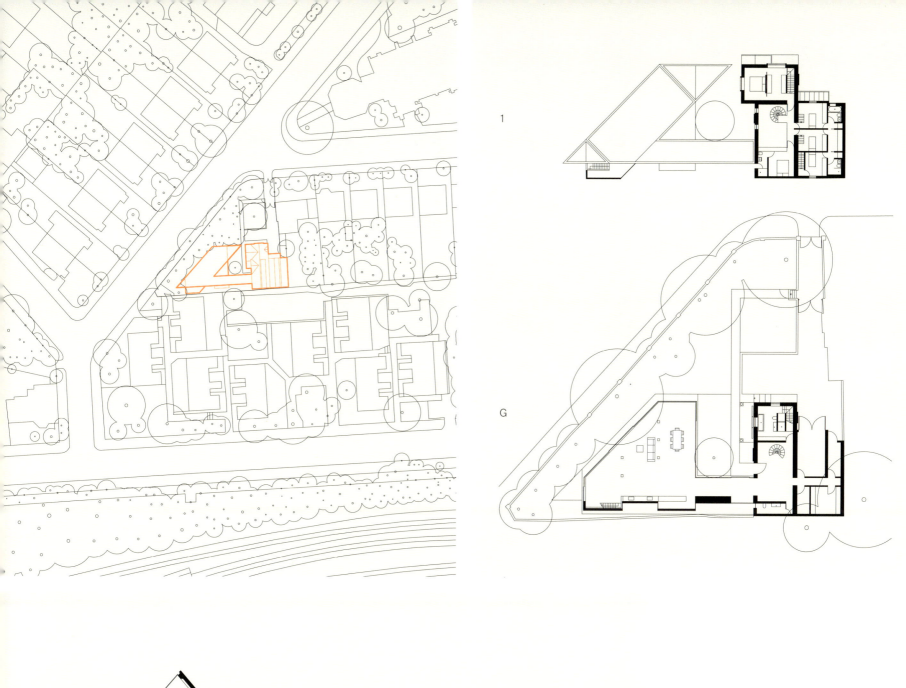
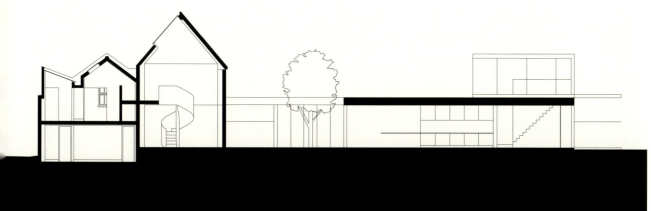

RENEW 115

RIGHT The plywood staircase is set within the double-height entrance hall within the Victorian house and leads to bedrooms at the upper level.

116 UNIQUE HOUSES

the warmer months. In terms of the planning process, which was time-consuming given that the house is in a Conservation Area, the practice was helped by references and allusions to the historic glasshouses that once sat on the site.

'When we are talking to the planners and the local community, we will always try and find something within the site itself that means the project relates back in some way to what was there before', says Eldridge. 'So the fact that we were putting a modern glasshouse onto the site and that it was subservient, at least in height, to the main house did create a strong argument in our favour. Also, having achieved planning consent for The Lawns, which was also quite radical for a Conservation Area, did help us in Conservation Areas in other parts of North London and sat well with the theme of reinventing buildings rather than trying to knock them down. The idea that we were also prepared to restore the original house faithfully gave us another important advantage.'

The new addition was softened further with a sedum roof, while a very slim first-floor element against a boundary wall offers a small study with the feeling of a tree house or lookout station. Given the openness of so much of the ground floor, this small but enticing room becomes an elegant escape pod looking out over the green roof to the garden beyond.

'The new addition has no partitions in it at all,' Eldridge says, 'and the ground floor of the old house is now also very open plan. So, as well as the bedrooms upstairs in the Victorian building, this is somewhere to retreat to when you want to just step away for a moment. But having decided to create this floating room, we then needed to make sure that the roof of the pavilion felt like a garden in itself, rather than something blank with pipes sticking out of it, which is so often the case. And we would usually look at the design of the roof as a way of trying to add biodiversity through planting, which also introduces some natural beauty. It works well with Jinny Blom's design, too, with the waving grasses and plants coming right up to the glass walls.'

Achieving this sense of transparency while avoiding internal partitions and structural walls meant a good deal of inventive engineering, with just four steel columns and cross braces holding up the cleverly designed stressed-skin roof structure – which in turn enabled the cantilever of the triangular canopy over the courtyard entrance. One other advantage of placing all of the communal family living spaces within the new addition was the way in which the pressure to maximise every square inch of space in the original part of the house was gently reduced. This can be seen, in particular, within the generously proportioned and double-height entrance hallway, accessed via the semi-protected courtyard. Here a large skylight enhances the richness of the space and illuminates a spiral staircase that serves as a dramatic focal point. This dynamic element, combined with the luxury of open space, creates an enticing statement room at the heart of the house that might also be used for entertaining.

'It was quite an extravagant use of space, especially in North London, and a brave move by the clients', says Eldridge. 'The staircase has always been an important element in our interiors: fun to design and with the capacity to create sculptural impact within a space, whether it is in an old building or a new one. It is a signature feature, and we designed a system using CNC-cut plywood treads that were then threaded over a central structural post, the loads then being transferred through each tread down to the ground. It was prototyped for the Hampstead house (see pages 128–137) and was developed with some variations for subsequent projects where a cost-effective solution was required.'

There is also room for service and storage spaces on the ground floor of the Victorian coachman's house and coach store, while upstairs there is room for five bedrooms. Even though the windows in this part of the house are smaller, and the children's bedrooms are relatively modest in size, this does not seem to matter when there is such a sense of openness to the ground floor and the new pavilion.

'It's actually rather lovely to have a house where there is that sense of difference between the types of space', Eldridge says. 'So you can retreat into the old house and the bedrooms if you wish, but even being in the glass house in the winter is quite wonderful because it is warm and protected but you still have the beauty of the courtyard and the garden. So that mix of spaces works really well.'

'There is this wonderful contrast between the original house, with its more private spaces, and the open family space', Seema Perez says. 'That was always the intention. And the garden is truly amazing. We got married three months after moving into the house and the wedding list was our garden – all the trees, plants, flowers. So the garden was a wedding gift from all our family and friends and it's something we can enjoy every day.'

ABOVE The cantilevered structure of the open-plan family space provides uninterrupted views of the garden and courtyard.

# HOUSE IN CHELSEA
# LONDON

The retrofitting and reinvention of period terraced houses offers a particular set of challenges when it comes to the creation of a welcoming 21st-century home. This is particularly true in certain parts of London, where the streetscape is tightly packed and outside space is in short supply. Such was the case with this Chelsea townhouse, which sits in a highly desirable neighbourhood but was relatively short on staples such as natural light and outside space. Nick Eldridge's clients acquired the building, which had sat empty for some time, knowing that there were multiple issues that needed to be addressed.

'Setting aside the condition of the house itself, there was a huge staircase that cut through a significant portion of every floor', say the clients, who have also been working with the practice on the update of their mill house in rural Wiltshire. 'The house is narrow but tall, so it was a case of trying to overcome this feeling of darkness and a sense of the walls closing in and, given that the building is so narrow, also the question of how to fit in all the necessary storage space.'

The house had been refurbished during the 1990s, but without much success. The only outside space had been swallowed up by a conservatory alongside the outrigger to the rear, holding the kitchen, while there were multiple changes in floor level throughout, which added to the disjointed character of the interiors within this tight, urban site just 5 metres (16½ feet) wide. The design process began with an exercise to try and strip away the failures of the previous refurbishment in the search for a comprehensive set of design solutions that would ultimately transform the building.

'These projects are all about making the most of small spaces', says Nick Eldridge. 'In this case the house was in a very poor state and the clients did consider knocking the whole thing down and just retaining the front facade until

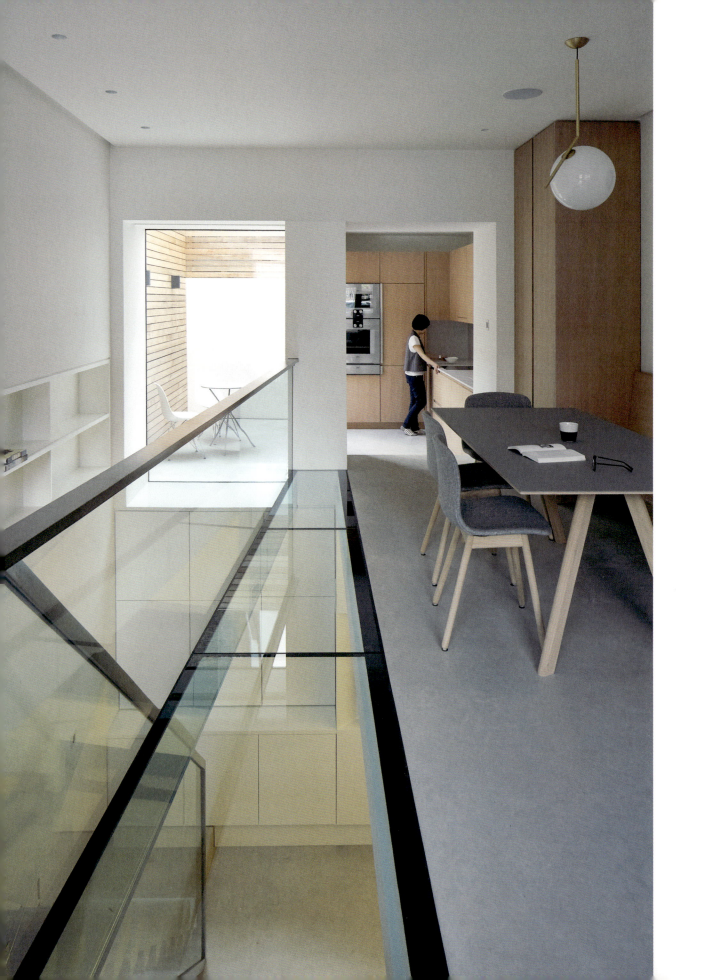

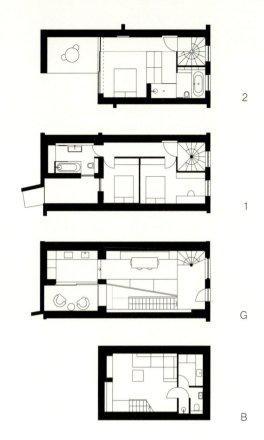

PAGE 121 This narrow house in Chelsea is transformed by the creation of a light-filled basement living space and the carefully selected neutral palette of materials throughout.

OPPOSITE The ground floor kitchen and dining areas are visually linked to the lower living area by a glass floor and gallery.

ABOVE Floor plans

RIGHT Cross section

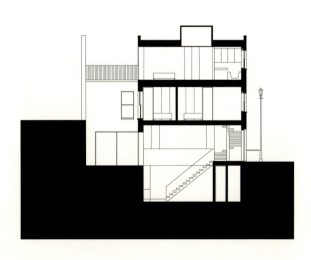

deciding to undertake a major refurbishment, which was a faster and less costly solution. Even then, anything associated with the party walls and the external envelope is of interest to the planners and the neighbours, so obtaining planning consent can be a struggle even when the house is not listed.'

The practice and its clients were helped in this case by the discovery of a half-height cellar, which had been fully enclosed and sealed off. This opened up the possibility of an enlarged basement level and a significant increase to the available living space, turning the house into a four-storey building. As well as holding utility spaces, including showers and other amenities for the couple's dogs, this new basement level was devoted to a spacious sitting room with natural light drawn in from a double-height lightwell. This was created by the introduction of a cantilevered stairway, with glass balustrades, complemented by a ribbon of structural glass flooring that runs alongside it. Banks of storage were also placed around the walls of the sitting room, while bookshelves were set into the side wall alongside the staircase.

Taken together, these ideas helped to liberate the plan of the ground floor. This became a fluid and open space with a dining area leading down to the remodelled kitchen extension, which now leads through not to a conservatory but to a courtyard that serves as a precious outdoor room. Banks of floor-to-ceiling glass on two sides of this courtyard illuminate not only the kitchen itself but also the ground floor and add to the quality of daylight spilling down into the sitting room.

'We wanted to create this sense of light and space, while leaving as much square footage as open as possible', say Eldridge's clients, who split their time between town and country. 'One of the most successful elements of the redesign is the use of glass and natural light to create these open spaces throughout the house. But we also wanted a "wow factor", and this idea of creating spaces that you might not necessarily expect to find when you look at the outside of the house.'

The use of oak and oak-ply joinery on the ground floor, in particular, helps to warm and soften the space while contrasting with the pale concrete and plaster. Bespoke elements include the timber banquette and storage cupboards in the dining area, the kitchen units and also timber cladding for the boundary walls in the courtyard. Another key feature here is the spiral staircase, made of laminated oak plywood, which reaches up to the first and second floors. This space-saving second stairway offers a rounded and sculptural element in an otherwise linear setting, but

LEFT The repositioning of the stair was key to the efficient use of space in the remodelling of this narrow house. This bespoke staircase is formed from CNC-cut oak-faced plywood and links the ground floor with the bedrooms on the two upper storeys.

RENEW 125

LEFT View from the kitchen to the street entrance.

BELOW The design of a staircase is often an opportunity to add a sculptural element within otherwise rectilinear space.

126 UNIQUE HOUSES

also serves as an additional lightwell, top-lit by a rooflight, and a ventilation stack that draws warm air to the top floor in the summer months before venting it outside.

'The position of the spiral staircase towards one corner at the front was important, as it is not using up valuable floor area', says Eldridge. 'With period terraced houses you often find that the staircase and landings are eating into living spaces, and you cannot afford to do that on a narrow site like this. So we have this very compact staircase to the upper floors but it also introduces natural light through the rooflight as well as working with the windows on the street frontage.'

Two bedrooms are situated on the first floor, along with a bathroom above the kitchen contained in the outrigger. The top storey is devoted to a spacious master suite that spills out, via a sliding wall of glass, onto a roof terrace that offers another hidden and secluded outdoor room.

'In London you just want to grasp every opportunity you can for your own outside space,' say Eldridge's clients, 'so the terraces were extremely important to us. With the glass walls and wooden panelling, the ground-floor terrace doesn't really feel that enclosed and we have an outside table there. The top-floor terrace can only be accessed through the master bedroom and it's this wonderful private space that's not overlooked by anyone. It also gets the sun all through the day.'

At the same time the envelope of the house was fully upgraded, with extensive insulation throughout. A combination of a heat-recovery ventilation system and underfloor heating means that the temperature of the house is well regulated but energy costs are kept low, with the project meeting a high standard in terms of environmental performance and sustainability.

Given the many constraints and limitations of the site itself, the kind of extensions and additions that the practice had explored in projects such as the reinvention of a period Victorian house in Hampstead (see pages 128–137) were not possible here. Yet, with the addition of a new basement level, lightwells and modest outside spaces – combined with fluid spaces and a wealth of integrated storage – the redesign of this terraced home has still been transformative for its owners.

'We wanted something special from the house and we were really drawn to Nick for his modern and uncompromising approach', say the clients. 'There wasn't anything that we thought was missing in the design – it fitted our brief, and more, while managing to be unique. It instantly felt like home to us.'

# HOUSE IN HAMPSTEAD LONDON

Following on from the success of The Lawns (see pages 98–109), Nick Eldridge and his practice began to receive a number of enquiries from potential clients in Hampstead, Highgate and other neighbouring 'villages' of North London, such as Belsize Park. These included a commission for a family home for rare-book dealer Bernard Shapero and his wife Emma, who works in the publishing industry, following a recommendation from Frances and John Sorrell, the clients at The Lawns. The Shaperos had come across a rare opportunity to buy a derelict, four-storey Victorian house in Hampstead, sitting between the high street and the Heath. More than this, the property came with a pair of 1930s garages alongside it that offered the golden possibility of extending and enlarging the house.

'It hadn't been lived in for 20 years when we bought it, which is incredible in a beautiful street like this', Emma Shapero said just after the project was completed. 'Because the house had been empty for so long, every original feature had been stripped out and you couldn't even see the lower-ground floor, which was all boarded up. But also the street itself has this quirkiness to it, with lots of different kinds of architectural styles, so we decided that we could be bold and do something interesting here rather than just reproducing Victoriana.'

When the Shaperos bought the site, they had one young child and were thinking about the need to provide more living space for the family than their old house, a few miles to the west, would allow. Given that the planning process was time-consuming, and slowed down by a small number of local objections, the couple had three children by the time they moved in. The Shaperos were glad to discover that Nick Eldridge and his former co-principal Piers Smerin also had young children at that point, with a welcome degree of understanding for the needs of a young family.

**128** UNIQUE HOUSES

PAGE 129 The practice is known for its bold juxtaposition of light-filled contemporary extensions with period houses in conservation areas. The link between the two is expressed here by a full-height window and roof light.

RIGHT The Victorian house and single-storey garage, which provided the opportunity for a contemporary extension.

OPPOSITE The enigmatic form of the three-storey extension affords privacy from the street.

'They had a sense of empathy for life with young kids,' said Emma Shapero, 'but at the same time we all wanted to do something that was as pared down as a family home can be. We wanted it to be practical but to have some elegance around us, without being surrounded by multicoloured toys all day. When we talked to our garden designer, Jinny Blom, we asked for something that was all about minimalism meeting wilderness and having this slightly crazy feeling contained by strict boundaries. It was the same sort of thing with the house: the wildness of our young family contained in this very calming space.'

The single-storey garages offered a tempting gap in the streetscape ready to be filled, but also seemed to mark a kind of punctuation mark between the aesthetic styles of the houses to either side of them. With this in mind, it seemed apposite to close the gap with a new addition that had a distinctive and contemporary character of its own, which would add valuable living space for the family but also offer a vibrant contrast with the updated Victorian villa. This juxtaposition of old and new may have slowed down the planning process, but it was also a key element of the project as a whole.

**130** UNIQUE HOUSES

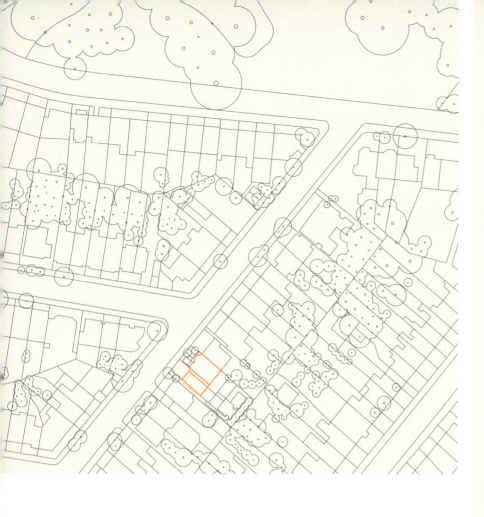

2

1
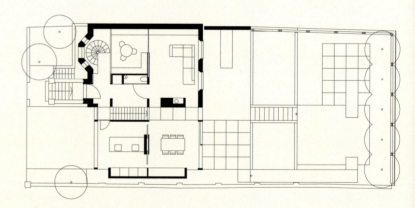
G
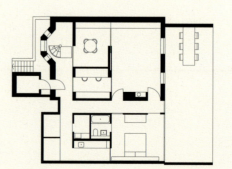
B

**132** UNIQUE HOUSES

'If you extend a house, you do want to give that extension a certain character that you don't have in the old,' says Nick Eldridge. 'So the project was about restoring the old Victorian building but also producing this light-filled and relatively open-plan space, so you now have a nice contrast between the cosier rooms to one side and the larger family spaces to the other. It's not just an extension, but something transformative.'

The new addition is slightly lower than the master building, with three storeys connecting with the lower-ground, ground and first floors of the period villa. There is a slim and respectful gap between its structure and the neighbours', where modest projecting lenses from the side elevation draw in light, while the practice also introduced a vertical ribbon of glass between the old and new parts of the extended house. From the street, this ribbon reads as an illuminated slot of frosted glass forming part of the contemporary facade, which is both linear and relatively enclosed, with sheets of birch-ply cladding interrupted further by just one slot window at ground-floor level and a brise-soleil around a larger window at first-floor level. Inside, this frosted-glass ribbon hosts the principal staircase, also made of glass, which is lit by a skylight at the top of the new structure.

'The transparent glass strip is a really important part of the design and an expression of the inter-space between old and new', Eldridge says. 'The fact that there is no real uniformity in the street allowed us to do something different in that space that is uncompromisingly modern yet also quite polite. It's quite an abstract composition but also gives you a secure feeling; you can open the windows to get some fresh air and ventilation but still feel protected from the street outside.'

The extension also helps to secure and shelter the rear garden, which becomes a private realm well suited to a family with children. Eldridge hung a 'floating' terrace off the back of the new addition – with a ramp in steel mesh running down to the garden itself, offering a choice of outdoor rooms complemented by Blom's landscaping and planting.

Moving inside, much of the lower-ground floor was devoted to the children and a nanny's bedroom suite or guest accommodation, as well as services and storage. This meant that the ground floor was freed up, with a living room and adjoining library in the old portion of the house – along with the main entrance – and a spacious kitchen and dining area in the new part, leading out to the 'floating'

OPPOSITE Floor plans and concept sketch illustrating the glass slot between the old and the new and the horizontal linkage between kitchen-dining and living space.

terrace. For Bernard Shapero, in particular, the library was an important element, featuring integrated bookshelves, storage and display units. It was designed in such a way that a sliding door could be easily drawn across to separate the space from the living room alongside, offering a degree of flexibility that was replicated at other points in the dwelling. Similarly, the use of integrated and custom-designed storage and furniture throughout the house maximised all available space while enhancing the sense of cohesion and reducing visual clutter.

On the first floor, two children's bedrooms sit in the old section of the house while the master suite takes up the new part, offering the parents a degree of independence. Another two bedrooms sit on the uppermost level of the villa, accessed by a spiral stairway. In total, then, the enlarged house features six bedrooms while still accommodating generously scaled communal spaces – with floor-to-ceiling banks of glass in the new extension dissolving some of the boundaries between inside and outside, enhancing the sense of openness.

Architecturally, the house manages to balance the need for the integration of the internal living spaces and floor plans across the Victorian villa and the contemporary addition, while maintaining a respectful sense of separation between the old and the new as seen from outside the building. The house and the streetscape are both enriched, but the demarcation lines in terms of aesthetics are clearly maintained rather than blurred or diminished in any way.

Although the Shaperos have since moved on, the house was a marked success for them and for their children: 'It was very important to Nick and Piers that everything was done to perfection, and we found the precision of their work really appealing', said Emma Shapero. 'They tried to think about everything that we might need, and the extension was just a fantastic solution that brings light flooding into the house.'

OPPOSITE A structural glass staircase allows natural light to filter through to the lower garden level spaces below.

136 UNIQUE HOUSES

ABOVE The kitchen and dining space in the new extension is linked to the remodelled Victorian house and opens out onto a terrace overlooking the garden. Privacy from the street is maintained by the narrow slot window in the front wall.

OPPOSITE The library and study is an essential element of the house for rare-book dealer Bernard Shapero.

# HOUSE IN NOTTING HILL
# LONDON

Modern manners and 21st-century patterns of living inevitably lead us towards homes that offer fluid, open and informal spaces with a rich quality of natural light and open connectivity to outdoor rooms, terraces and gardens. Yet the Victorian townhouses that still make up a significant proportion of our urban building stock, often in highly desirable settings, rarely offer such characteristics without a significant process of reinvention and retrofitting. Traditionally, such houses offered a very formal and cellular collection of rooms, while their relationship to gardens and outside space was limited by load-bearing brick walls. Modern extensions and upgrades, usually on the rear elevation of such buildings, look to create free-flowing family spaces that also make the most of any precious outdoor areas. Such was the case with this Victorian house in Notting Hill.

The clients, who work in the finance industry and have three children, came to the practice at the recommendation of the owners of a period townhouse in Chelsea (see pages 120–127), which had also been reinvented by Eldridge London. The Notting Hill house had last been refurbished in the 2000s by a bachelor who, understandably, had not given any thought to the kind of spaces that a young family might need – and the result was that the layout of the four-storey dwelling was still dominated by a cellular floor plan throughout.

'The previous owner had spent a lot of money on upgrading the building but without thinking much about how to live in these spaces in a more contemporary way', says Mike Gibson. 'There wasn't much of a relationship with the garden and there wasn't much sense of connection between the different floor levels either – particularly between the ground and lower-ground floors, where the staircase was totally enclosed and separated those spaces. What the clients really wanted to do was to open it all up, so that there was more life to the interiors.'

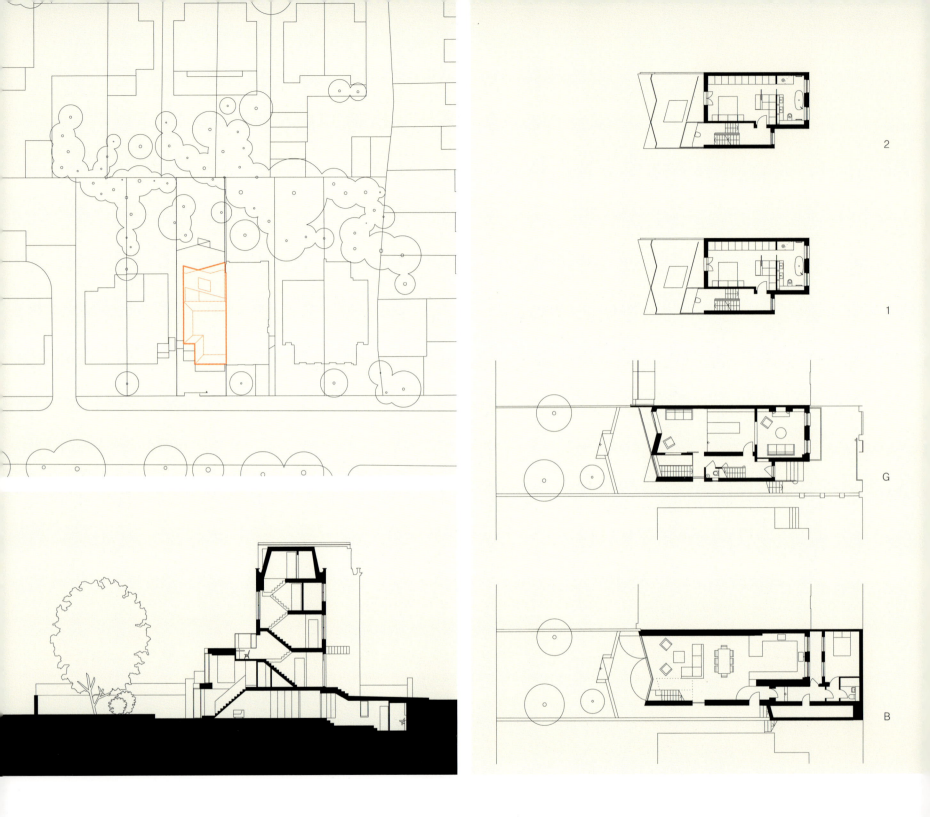

ABOVE Floor plans and cross-section.

140 UNIQUE HOUSES

Much of the energy within the project was focused on the two lower levels and the rear garden. The design process involved a careful analysis of neighbouring buildings, looking at the form and mass of other extensions along with their fenestration. Privacy was always going to be a key issue, not just for the family itself but also for the residents living alongside within the same row of terraced houses. Mike Gibson and Nick Eldridge looked at various ideas for a transformative addition at the back of the house, before stepping away from the linear blocks tagged onto many other residences here and embracing something more dynamic. Taking sight lines into account, the practice developed a more angular profile for an addition that would span and connect the ground and lower-ground floors.

'The clients wanted to do something special, but the difficulty of working in Conservation Areas like this is that if you do present something that looks and feels different then the conservation officers start to raise their eyebrows and you might get objections from the neighbours', says Gibson. 'So we tried to find a way of doing something interesting and specific to the family, while working within an envelope that was clearly referential and reverential to the neighbouring houses and very much in context. What we came up with made it very difficult for the conservation officers to say that it didn't fit in, because the design was so directly related to the sight lines of the neighbours in a way that protects their privacy as well.

'What we have always enjoyed as a practice is having quite a rigorous geometric approach combined with finding something in the site itself that gives a structure or order to things. Here the clients were interested in doing something a little bit more interesting and, from our side, exploring an angular, 15-degree geometry offered us a framework in which we could do something quite playful.'

Angling the rear walls and windows in such a considered manner became the key element in terms of achieving a design that was not only more dynamic and engaging than typical rear extensions but also created vital opportunities to enhance the inside–outside relationship with banks of floor-to-ceiling glass. On the lower-ground floor, the angled glass doors fold back to allow an almost seamless transition between inside and out, with the family lounge spilling out onto a sunken terrace in the garden. Landscaping around the terrace offers integrated planters with retaining walls that double as benches, meaning that this fresh-air

PAGE 139 Night view of the extension to this Notting Hill Victorian house creating additional living space with access to the garden.

space becomes a valuable outdoor room – which also helps to enrich the sense of openness, space and light within the house itself.

Inside, an open-plan layout creates a new family hub, with the lounge flowing through to the dining area and then the kitchen beyond without any partition walls between these zones. There was also an opportunity to create an extra bedroom suite, discreetly tucked under the modest front garden, which might suit a nanny or guests.

On the upper-ground floor, the arrangement to the front of the house is relatively formal – with the main entrance hall and principal staircase to one side and a snug to the other. But, beyond this, the practice was able to carry the main reception room, which serves as a sitting room and library, out into the new extension. This enlarged and revitalised space now looks out over the rear garden via a large window that slides open to allow access to a slim balcony with a glass balustrade.

Another important aspect of the design is the new staircase that connects these two levels. It was vital that this element did not start swallowing up living space, as had been the case with the previous floor plan of the house – so it now cantilevers out from the party wall to one side. Yet the practice was still able to turn the stairway into a feature in its own right by using characterful, custom-made limestone steps. With each one cut from a single block of stone, the distinctive angular geometry of these 'floating' risers subtly echoes the triangular shapes of the rear elevation.

'With the staircase, which is made of Moleanos limestone from Portugal, we started talking about coordinating the alignment of the steps with the new building, as well as referencing Soane-ian cantilevered staircases,' says Gibson, 'and the clients really bought into it. It's taking quite a traditional idea and then bringing it into the 21st century.

'It is a standout piece, but what's interesting is that when you arrive at the house on the upper-ground floor and step down through this double-height void to the open space below, you don't really understand the shape of the staircase until you turn back and see it. It's only then that you get this reveal and see how all the stone treads are cantilevered off the wall and how light the whole thing seems to be. So it becomes quite a surprise.'

LEFT Top-lit sitting space with views to the garden.

OPPOSITE  The natural limestone facade of the extension is set at angles relating to the sight lines of the neighbours to maintain privacy.

RIGHT The limestone staircase, which connects the two levels of the extension cantilevers from the wall, the tread geometry echoing the angular form of the new building.

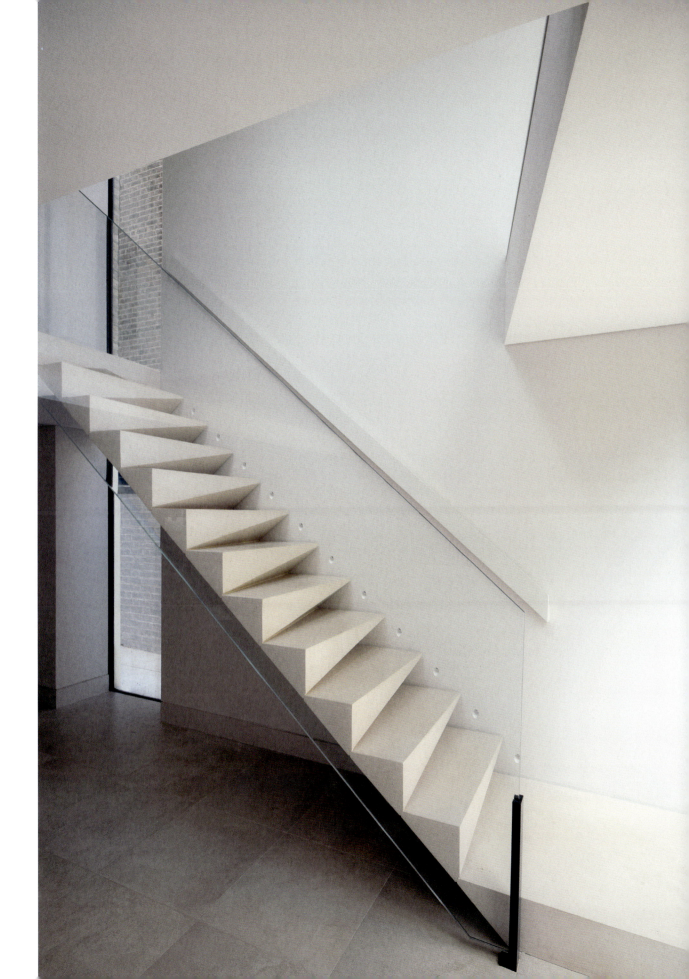

RIGHT The angular facade is accentuated by sunlight washing the surfaces of the limestone cladding.

Given the nature of the *promenade architecturale* through the old part of the house and into the new, as well as down and out into the open-plan living area and garden, the new extension as a whole is revelatory. The journey is lent impetus and energy by a series of enticing surprises. At the same time, of course, the welcoming openness of the spaces themselves – particularly on the lower-ground floor – make them well suited to family living.

'It's a project that's trying to push the boundaries in design terms but there is this element of logic that comes out of the brief and out of the site', says Nick Eldridge. 'So there is nothing purely wilful about it and these points of inspiration, or drivers, come from the specific contexts of each project.

'But obviously we do want to make a building memorable and it needs to have a strong material quality as well, so material and form always go hand in hand. The limestone cladding on the rear elevation and for the stairs is really beautiful, and it's a testament to Mike that we achieved that level of finish. It's not a cheap solution but it has a real sense of quality and character to it.'

# BARN IN NEWLYN
# CORNWALL

It was an interest in art, and the work of Terry Frost in particular, that first brought Nick Eldridge to the westernmost tip of England. He had, for some years, collected prints by Frost and was then introduced to him by mutual friends – namely, John and Frances Sorrell, who commissioned the practice to design their home, The Lawns, in Highgate (see pages 98–109). Terry Frost lived and worked in Cornwall periodically from the 1940s all the way through to his death in 2003, savouring the quality of the light there and being part of a long-established community of painters and artists.

'The Sorrells collected Frost's work and had a large painting of his called *Through Blues*, for which one wall of the new entrance hall of The Lawns had to be specifically built,' says Eldridge. 'They suggested that I should meet him, so on a trip with my family we enjoyed some time with him in his studio in Newlyn, followed by tea in the house with his wife, before returning to the Penzance Arts Club in Chapel Street where we were staying. I was inspired by Terry Frost's brightness and optimism which is also so evident in his work.'

Frost was one of many artists associated with Newlyn, St Ives and Penwith. The Newlyn School was an art colony founded by Walter Langley and others during the late 19th century, focused on this fishing village not far from Penzance. There were multiple temptations for artists at that time, including the light and the landscape but also the sense of quiet and solitude – as well as the affordability of houses and outbuildings that could easily be adapted into painting studios. Many of these attractions remain, of course, even if the fishing fleets that once fascinated the Newlyn School have diminished and property prices have climbed and climbed. For Eldridge, the end-of-the-line feeling within West Penwith, combined with its artistic and creative heritage, were especially alluring – and the region remained in his mind long after his first visit to Newlyn to meet Terry Frost.

PAGE 149 The new entrance porch projects out into the garden to create a more generous arrival space. The large glazed panel looks out onto a planter raised above the level of the bedrock and a Cornish hedge constructed from reclaimed and new granite from a local quarry.

LEFT The third barn has been converted into a studio with a mezzanine within the reconstructed roof volume. The oak and plywood glazing system was designed by the architect and prefabricated and installed by a furniture maker based in Sussex.

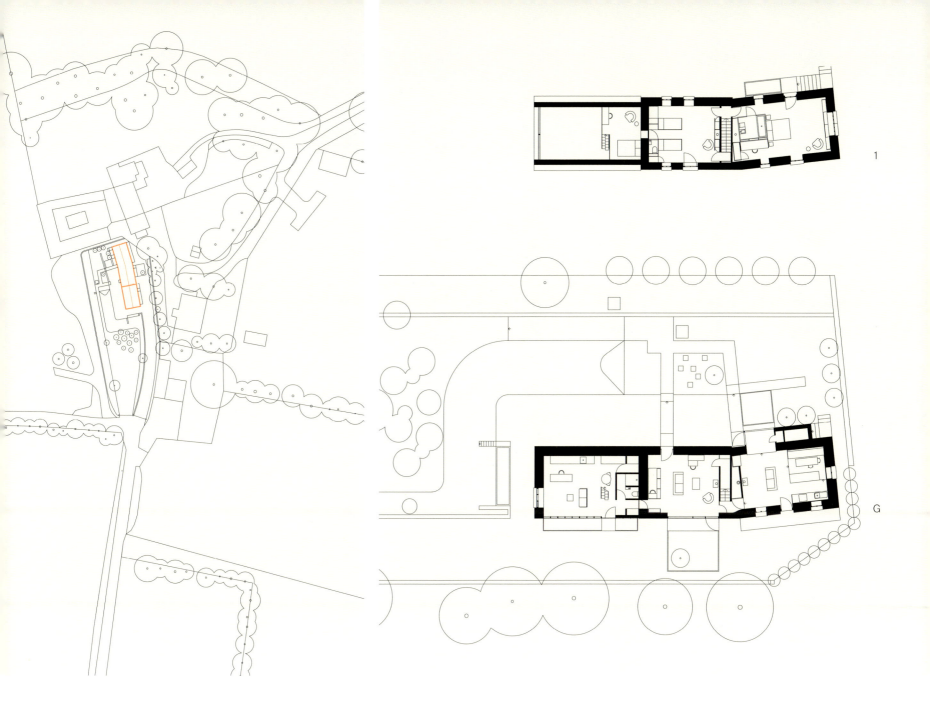

OPPOSITE The changes in the garden levels are the result of a metre-depth of soil being removed from the west wall of the three interlinked barns. In the porch the Peahen, which arrived at the start of lockdown, takes shelter.

ABOVE Location and floor plans.

'In 2008 I embarked upon a printmaking course at Heatherley's in London,' says Eldridge, 'and, inspired by Ben Nicholson's work, I visited Tate St Ives and decided that it would be refreshing to establish a studio for working on projects in the south-west. It took two years before finding a derelict barn that could be converted into a studio and also a place to stay. The south side of the peninsula was more affordable and I preferred the industrial quality of Newlyn as a working fishing port in contrast to St Ives, which appeared subsumed by tourism. The barn, although at the top of a hill, was a relatively short cycling distance from Penzance station with a train journey of five and a half hours to Paddington. But, in a sense, it was the idea of being more than 300 miles [almost 500 km] from London that added to the appeal of the region for me.'

The key element within this gradual shift towards the West Country – where Eldridge has established a satellite studio to the London office, known as Eldridge Newlyn – is the converted barn. Dating back to the early 1800s, it is part of a larger farmstead that once included the nearby farmhouse, notably rented by the painter Sir Alfred Munnings when he arrived in Cornwall in 1908, a few years before he became a member of the Newlyn School; he later became President of the Royal Academy.

The other great temptation of the barn for Eldridge, as an architect, was the golden opportunity that it offered to experiment and develop fresh ideas while working on his own project. The main part of the building had possibly been used as a threshing barn and then as a stable block. At some point the timber structure that separated two floors at one end of the building had rotted, but the barn had at least been re-roofed by the former owner – who had also managed to acquire planning permission to convert it to residential use before selling the farm and its surrounding fields.

Having bought the barn, it made sense to convert the older, taller part of the building into residential accommodation arranged over two floors, while Eldridge decided to adapt the later and slightly lower addition at one end into the studio. This is a largely double-height room, with the exception of a modest mezzanine gallery that serves as a study and bed space. One of the benefits of this arrangement is that it allows the creation of a healthy distinction between work and home, with a sense of separation between the two realms along with dedicated entrances to both on opposite sides of the building.

LEFT The walls of the studio, kitchen units and prototype sofa are in birch-faced plywood. The floor is a tightly laid grid of kiln bricks. The print on the wall is by Terry Frost, who lived nearby.

RENEW 153

ABOVE The bathroom pod is one of a number of prefabricated structures in the barn designed to sit independently of the lime-plastered granite walls that maintain their original uneven lines. A desk space is integrated into the back of the pod. The upper level floors are in birch plywood.

Eldridge adopted a common approach to both home and studio in terms of his choice of materials, as well as an emphasis on a soothing palette of natural textures and finishes. It was important to him, from the outset, to use natural and local materials as far as possible, which relates not only to questions of sustainability but also to context and the elemental character of West Penwith.

'I started exploring locally,' says Eldridge, 'and discovered that I could buy large slabs of granite at Trenoweth Quarry in Mabe, and this is such a beautiful stone. Not far from that quarry is a sawmill processing local oak and Douglas fir. Local materials are more costly than imported granite from Portugal, for example, but the purist within took me to back to the local stone. Although the floors were originally meant to be in Douglas fir, I wanted to limit the palette of materials – so I decided to replace the floor structures with oak beams and joists, which would also match the joinery of the new windows that were also made with oak for durability.'

The granite walls, which vary between 500 and 700 mm (20 and 28 inches) in thickness, are lime-plastered and unpainted, so the intrinsic character of the material shines through. The natural plaster is a soft grey, which also has a perfect tonal relationship with the oak, brick floors and birch plywood – the other three key materials that define the project.

'For the floor in the studio and the house, I wanted a hard surface because Cornwall's climate is very wet', says Eldridge. 'Inspired by Carl Andre's famous *Equivalent VIII* installation of bricks that was exhibited at the Tate in 1974, I chose to use firebricks that I had also seen in the kilns of the Leach Pottery in St Ives. The bricks are precise with very square edges, which enabled me to have them laid with tight, dry joints exactly as you see in Andre's work. There were no cut bricks, with the idea that the gap between the floor and the irregular walls would be expressed.'

This approach connected with Eldridge's idea that any new elements of the interior would be clearly fresh and precise – establishing a vivid contrast with the decidedly imprecise shell of the existing building, which was faithfully restored with traditional materials and detailing. These new elements and insertions within the barn, including the fitted furniture, read as modern and contemporary installations juxtaposed with the old and irregular fabric of the building.

'With your own projects, you can be a little more experimental,' says Eldridge, 'and if it doesn't work you can just say "I wouldn't do that again". At first, I was unable to find any makers in the region who could work accurately with plywood, so I worked with a furniture maker in East Grinstead, who has produced some wonderful pieces of joinery for our projects for over 15 years. The long distance between West Sussex and Cornwall meant that all the plywood components were designed to be flat-packed, test fitted in the workshop and then brought down to West Penwith for assembly.'

Because of the irregularity of the walls of the 200-year-old barn and the desire to retain the open volumes into the roof space, Eldridge developed a series of free-standing plywood furniture pods – including bed pods, a bathroom pod and a work pod up on the first floor. Having been inspected in the workshop, the plywood bathroom pod was brought in as four walls, a lid and floor with water-proof, white-Corian floor and wall linings around the bath. The lid included a hatch that, when open, lets light flood into the cube from a skylight in the roof. It was assembled in the bedroom space in a day, providing an oasis of perfection while work on the house continued all around it.

'I also managed to persuade Joe, our joiner, to take on the manufacture of the entire external wall of my studio', says Eldridge. 'This was made with a birch-plywood framework internally and oak externally, and then installed over a four-day period together with the glazing, which they also brought with them in the van. The glazing system we designed consists of 600 mm (23½ inch) wide vertical panels of glass, which proved to be cheaper than the large glazed panels that we would normally specify for our clients' houses. The vertical rhythm of the narrower panels of glass is very beautiful and lets wonderful morning sunlight into the studio. To save on costs, none of the glazed panels opens – so instead we installed a solid shutter and door to ventilate the space or to walk outside. This breaks with the convention of sliding doors, but in this climate and for a studio the design works very well and, as a successful prototype, it's something that I will develop for other projects.'

The soft colours of the brick, plaster, ply and timber create a calming quality throughout, while underfloor heating avoids the need for radiators; the water for these underfloor coils is warmed by electric power, soon to be provided by a solar array situated in a nearby field. Many bespoke elements within the interiors of the residential portion of the barn are in birch ply, including the custom kitchen units,

RIGHT The original floors of the barn had rotted and were replaced with oak beams and joists to a traditional design. The three-metre-long bench is on a raised platform to the left of the kitchen island.

BELOW The plywood kitchen was designed by the architect, prefabricated in Sussex and assembled on site standing independently of the unpainted lime-plastered walls.

ABOVE The natural material palette consists of oak, kiln bricks, lime plaster, and birch-faced plywood and glass. External doors and windows are oak and internal doors are plywood. The door to the left leads into a comfortable sitting space and library and is linked to the studio beyond.

island and fitted settle alongside the dining table – all sitting on a slightly raised platform that ties the space together.

'We have had 14 people in that space around the table and the island, so it works really well for us', Eldridge says. 'The platform idea was partly inspired by the one that we designed for the kitchen at Greenways (see pages 20–35), so you can sit comfortably on one side of the island while others are cooking just on the other side of it, which is a very social way to entertain.'

The garden and landscaping have also been a labour of love. The area around the barn had been concreted over to serve as part of the farmyard, so all the concrete had to be broken up and, even then, the ground below is 'rab' – a subsoil of weathered granite and impenetrable bedrock. Planting holes had to be excavated for yews, which add all-year-round structure. Eldridge designed an elegant pathway that leads towards the house with a Cornish hedge of stone and earth to one side and a grass bank to the other, while stone walls also serve as a protective border around much of the garden, and a series of raised planters creates deeper beds for planting as there is little soil below. Such elements soften the setting but also help to draw out the elemental colour and character of the stone walls of the barn itself.

'It is certainly an elemental place,' says Eldridge, 'and the weather is so extreme. We enjoy a lot of sunshine in the summer but also get a lot of rain and winds off the Atlantic. So you need to be an enthusiast to happily survive here all year round. I have grown to love the region and its coastline, which is walking distance from here. It is a magical place for walking and swimming and, as the north and south coast are so near to each other, you can choose one or the other depending on the wind direction. When the tide is right you can swim before work, which is a wonderful way of waking up. I tend to get up with the sun and try to get to bed early, although I often enjoy working late into the night if there is a project with a deadline.'

In terms of the costs of conversion, Eldridge concedes that it would have been cheaper to build a new house from scratch. But that would have provided neither the character nor the history or patina that he finds so engaging here. 'There are some things that I could have also done more cheaply, but I just wanted to do something that I was really happy with and that was going to last', Eldridge says. 'And to my mind it's strange that there are still so many buildings like this that have really been underestimated.'

BELOW Model exhibited in the Royal Academy of Arts Summer Exhibition with the caption 'Architect Nick Eldridge grew up in this house in Kent and returns to build a new structure for his own family on the roof of the building where his parents still live. The Planning authority requires the new to be connected to the old.'

# AFTERWORD
# CHASING PERFECTION

This book has illustrated 12 houses that represent a cross section of the 50 residential projects we have designed since the practice was established in 1998. I hasten to add that not all of the 50 have been built, and that while we have been fortunate to have realised many beautiful houses, there are a few unbuilt designs that I have not yet given up on.

As a personal insight into where the thought processes and influences behind the houses and their design emanate, I have made a collection of paragraphs edited from a lengthy set of biographical notes in search of the answer to this question. With the realisation that most of life's experiences have some influence on our creative output, this has been a time-consuming process of abbreviation.

Nonetheless, if I were asked to define my aim as an architect, it would be 'chasing perfection'.

My mother, who studied and later taught textile design and dressmaking at art college in the 1950s, was by nature a perfectionist and was blessed with infinite patience. By contrast, my father, an art director in London advertising agencies, had little patience and was more interested in getting things done – fast. It was for this reason that he felt unsuited to being an architect, the profession that his father had encouraged him to pursue.

I inherited the propensity for perfectionism from my mother, and my level of patience lies somewhere between my two parents.

We moved to a symmetrical Victorian house in the Kent countryside when I was four years old. I look back on my childhood as being quite idyllic, always pursuing interests obsessively and developing a very clear sense of purpose early on. Without brothers and sisters, I was used to the company of adults and was perhaps considered a serious child as a result. At weekends, I would enjoy my father's company visiting antique shops, and I would be drawn to objects of all kinds for their craftsmanship and perfection. This culminated in a long-term interest in the most functional of objects, cutlery, which I used to collect. As a child visiting my cousins' house, I remember the Arne Jacobsen stainless-steel cutlery set out on their Fritz Hansen table, and sitting on three-legged Ant chairs. My uncle, a journalist on Fleet Street, had a remarkable sense of design, and their post-war house from the outside was traditional but quite radically modern on the inside – regrettably, he never talked about design.

My parents had a large circle of friends who were mainly doctors or artists, and it was the artists' houses that intrigued me. They led interesting, bohemian lives in half-timbered houses with rugs on bare floorboards. At private views, I would get lost in the crowds and wander the house. There were children there but they played in the roof, and instead I took an interest in the art and listened as people drank wine and purchases were made before they stumbled out onto the street and into their cars.

In the village near us lived a painter and sculptor and her husband, whose modern house had been designed by an architect. Set between traditional red-brick houses with Kent peg-tiled roofs was their brick and white-rendered house with large glass sliding doors onto terraces and sweeping lawns. There was a double-height space with open gallery overlooking the kitchen, and white walls with carefully placed paintings. They had Persian rugs, which were soft on the feet coming in from the pool, and they drank Earl Grey tea from simply designed putty-coloured Arabia cups, which I very much liked. She had a Vidal Sassoon haircut, an art studio suffused with the sweet smell of oil paint and a white Triumph Vitesse with a roof that would come down on our trips to the sea. Her husband worked in the metal exchange and commuted to London with my father each day. He drove a silver Reliant Scimitar, which had a wonderfully large and flat back window with a narrow stainless-steel frame that lifted unlike any other I had seen.

At school, I devoted most of my time to art and music – doing just enough on the other subjects to get by. After a number of years singing in concerts in and out of school and in the choirs of Canterbury Cathedral and St Margaret's, Westminster, my final performances were as the boy Miles in Scottish Opera's production of the *Turn of the Screw* by Benjamin Britten. My voice began to break, which coincided with my art master setting a project to design a building. He praised my design for an art gallery in London's Hyde Park, and at 13 my focus was redirected from music to thoughts of a career in architecture.

I left school and travelled through Europe with a school friend who was more interested in vintage motorbikes than art and architecture but was happy to accompany me in my search for buildings by Le Corbusier in France and villas by Palladio in Italy. My father had lent us his company van with his name on the side in large, black Helvetica letters – and as we drove through villages, people would wave and shout out my name.

When I returned, I found work in the offices of Chamberlin, Powell and Bon, the architects of the Barbican, and financed a trip to the Far East. I stayed with a school friend in Hong Kong whose father was the Minister for Culture and lived on the Peak. Most of the time was spent by the pool of their club, and I found little of particular interest although I appreciated their hospitality and the opportunity to see where they lived. After two weeks, I flew on to Japan. Landing in Tokyo was like landing on another planet, and it was all I could do to absorb the culture that would have a significant influence on my life and on my work from that time on. I stayed with a client of my father's who worked for Japan Airlines, living just outside Tokyo, and their parents and cousins lived in minka, the traditional Japanese houses of timber with shoji screens. On the same site, they had built for themselves a contemporary European-style house with white-rendered walls and a mono-pitched roof. After a week of exploring the vibrant districts of Tokyo – Shinjuku and Ginza – and the calm of the Imperial Palace, I was put on the Shinkansen bullet train to Kyoto and booked into a ryokan, a traditional Japanese inn with a room of tatami; bed on the floor; wooden soaking tub and shower; and small, magical Japanese garden and terrace beyond sliding doors. From here, I ventured through the old city of Kyoto and to the remarkable Zen-Buddhist Kinkaku-ji temple with its gold-leafed walls reflected in the ponds of the garden. I had learnt about the philosophy and meaning behind Japanese traditional architecture and landscape design – and had wondered why the Japanese of my generation craved the European style, which I felt to be superficial and fleeting. I had supposed it was a rebellion, a desire for independence, an escape from tradition – which, in many ways, I was intent upon too.

Back from my travels, I took up my place at the School of Architecture in Liverpool, which was a culture shock of a different kind but I established a close circle of architect friends and we worked in healthy competition for three years. Renzo Piano and Richard Rogers' Centre Pompidou had opened the year I arrived in Liverpool, and a trip to Paris to visit this building and the Maison de Verre had inspired the pursuit of lightweight steel-and-glass structures. The Maison de Verre of 1932 was a Gesamtkunstwerk where every part of the building, its interior and its furnishings were bespoke and the work of the designer Pierre Chareau, architect Bernard Bijvoet and metalworker Louis Dalbet. At Liverpool, I designed an imaginary house for the architect and teacher Cedric Price as it was an opportunity to meet someone whose ideas had influenced Piano and Rogers and a generation of architects when he had taught at the AA. His office was off Tottenham Court Road near the Building Centre. He referred to his private studio on the top floor above the office as 'East Grinstead', and in the days before mobile phones when in 'East Grinstead' he could be conveniently out of contact. He was very distinctive to look at. He wore blue shirts with white collars, and the collars had rounded corners – and he smoked a cigar, which was rarely out of his mouth. The interviews I conducted were entertaining, and more so towards the end of the day when he would offer me a brandy. As a teacher, he had a lot of advice – if a client gives you a site, then build a structure across every square inch of it. The hypothetical house I designed for him was probably far too tectonic for such a visionary, but tried to incorporate his theories of flexibility and the ever-changing environment. Set within an open volume, the living space was designed with movable, sliding and pivoting walls to create different plan forms and variable room functions; bathroom and kitchen modules were open or closed as free-standing furniture. Added to the notion of flexible space was the idea that the architect could design more than just the shell of a building but also the interior and the door handles and even the cutlery, which interested me then and still does. This, of course, was not a new idea as Le Corbusier and Gerrit Rietveld had done it all a half-century before. I had completed the degree course and had delivered a dissertation on purism, studying the work of Le Corbusier and Ozenfant, but technically I was not much further advanced and resolved to learn about insulation and waterproofing of buildings in the office. After all, Cedric Price had said, 'Technology is the answer, but what was the question?' On the eve of the results being posted on the school noticeboard, my tutor had told me that I would either fail or get a first, as if failure would have been the ultimate recognition for breaking rules and not quite fitting in, which was a philosophy that he actively encouraged. We all did well and returned to London to take up jobs and start new lives with other people, only meeting again not long enough after to attend the funeral of one of our group – perhaps the most talented and uncompromising of us all.

In London, I worked for Pentagram, a multi-disciplinary design company with offices overlooking Paddington, which one of the partners, the brilliant graphic designer Alan Fletcher, described as having one of the best views of East Germany in London. I had been interviewed by Archigram founder Ron Herron, but found myself working for Theo Crosby on corporate offices and the reconstruction of the Globe Theatre on Bankside as Herron had no work when I arrived. This wasn't quite what I had imagined, but I was living in London and the studio was full of young people of my age – but here I felt more observer than participant, as I didn't feel a great passion for this more eclectic style of architecture. Towards the end of my year, I asked to transfer to the office in New York for a month and flew across with a small portfolio of work under my arm. I had contacted a tutor from the US teaching at Liverpool, who introduced me to a former Oregon student of his working as features editor on an architectural magazine in New York. She had a loft apartment in Greenwich Village, and provided me with accommodation for the month and introduced me to the fashionable lifestyle of Lower Manhattan. In the Flatiron Building studio on Broadway and Fifth Avenue, Pentagram partner Colin Forbes asked me to produce a set of working details for an extension to his ranch in North Carolina. As a student, I had so little experience but felt unable to refuse. I talked it through with my friend that evening, and the next day she bought me a book on timber construction with details that helped me make convincing drawings of the ranch extension and which Forbes gratefully took to his builder.

I had written to architects in New York from London, and arranged interviews with the idea that I would perhaps delay the start of my diploma year and work longer in New York if an opportunity arose. Many had replied and I was interviewed by Philip Johnson, whose Glass House in New Canaan, Connecticut, inspired by Mies van der Rohe and the Farnsworth House, I had referenced as a student. I had recently walked past the impressive concrete frame of Johnson's new AT&T tower on Madison Avenue with its provocatively postmodern 'Chippendale' top. In his office, I showed Johnson the housing system that I had designed for infilling gaps in the derelict Georgian terraces of Toxteth, Liverpool 8, where I had been living. 'Vers une new terraced house' was a corruption of Le Corbusier's manifesto, *Towards a New Architecture*, and was a distillation of the art of living, questioning conservation and proposing contemporary infill with light-filled open-plan space behind fully glazed facades. I explained to Johnson that I knew it was ambitious but that it seemed to be a valid solution to the city problem. Johnson's response to the student who had travelled 3,000 miles looking for work was, 'without ambition you won't get anywhere'. He offered me a job but, like other celebrated architects in the 1980s, he wouldn't pay me. It was enough, however, that I had been inspired by the 74-year-old's energy and enthusiasm and the playful genius that had made the bold and iconic postmodern statement on Madison after pioneering modernism. I thanked him, left and flew back to London.

Returning from New York, London seemed like a village by comparison – and going back to Liverpool to start my fourth year felt like a step backwards. I began the term commuting from London for hand-ins and juries, taking the train back at the end of the day. I soon realised that I should continue my studies at the Architectural Association instead, and it was the timely opportunity to work for Norman Foster that enabled me to pay the AA school fees. My first job was on the site of the recently completed Renault building in Swindon, snagging the aluminium cladding from a cherry picker. During my diploma years in the office, I worked mainly on competitions in the UK and abroad.

At the Architectural Association, my tutor Ron Herron had said, 'Forget Foster and find your own style'. My work was conceptual but always tangible. In Herron's and Jan Kaplický's Unit 8, we always felt like outsiders. The students of Peter Cook, Zaha Hadid and Daniel Libeskind were examining the outer reaches of architecture and urban planning in a more holistic way, and it was more than a decade later that Hadid built her first building – her wall-sized paintings evolving eventually into very exciting, if crudely built, structures.

As a student of architecture, I had high ideals yet I was not particularly interested in writing about or conceptualising architecture. I did, however, carry a handful of inspirational books from one flat to the next – including the satisfyingly square, white book entitled *Five Architects,* first published in 1972, which I was given to look at by a tutor but never managed to return before I graduated. Of the work of the five architects it featured, it was John Hejduk's (unbuilt) House 10 that captivated me, such was the beauty of its composition. It is perhaps significant that Kenneth Frampton starts his section in the book with House 10, writing that 'it probably insists more than any other project here on a formal appraisal'. This is exactly how I responded to the 'hieroglyphic' drawings, as Frampton describes them: 'without legend or furniture it is impossible to know the program'. And this is what has fascinated me – the fact that lines on paper can insinuate a collection of interlinked forms with very minimal definition. In Hejduk's projects, I wonder if they were designed to exist primarily on paper in perfect isolation or whether there was an ambition to build them.

After graduating, I joined Herron and Kaplický as part-time technical tutor of their unit, and in the office I gained enough confidence to make contributions to the design reviews with Norman Foster and the project team. Foster liked the logic of a modular design that I had proposed for the extension of his IBM building at Greenford, as the brief from the client was unspecific and the design therefore needed to be flexible and allow for expansion. He allowed me to develop the idea with a small team, and it was at this point that the director in charge took me down to the basement meeting room and told me that 'the office is democratic but not that democratic'. I sidestepped the hierarchy two years later when Norman Foster approached my desk one morning and asked me to go to the South of France for a few weeks to organise some building work on a house that he had bought in the hills near Grasse. The few weeks became two years, of which one year was spent on the house and the second on Foster's Carré d'Art, the new Médiathèque in the centre of Nîmes, living in the heroic brut-concrete apartment building designed by Jean Nouvel. In the London office, I had had no detailed design experience – and so getting something built using my rusted school French was even more challenging, but enormously enjoyable for a young man in his late twenties living in the South of France. Working so closely with an architect of Norman Foster's genius is an opportunity that few student architects are given. Of course it was precarious, and I was warned by my friends in the office that I probably wouldn't last long working on the house as there was no room to hide – I was exposed, but why would I want to hide; I wanted to learn, and I did.

When the Nîmes office eventually closed and I returned to London, the Hong Kong team had also returned and it was a different place. I had been made an associate of the practice but it was time to leave; I joined Troughton McAslan, a young and up-and-coming practice in Notting Hill Gate. Here, in one interview, I transformed from student to project architect with a salary that enabled me to get a mortgage and afford to buy a house – albeit without a roof. I was responsible for the design of their second headquarters building for Apple at Stockley Park in West London, and with plenty of work in the office I was left to my own devices. The buildings on the business park were formulaic with strict rules, which I set about trying to break for a building design that was all glass; all white; without extraneous detail; and, of course, built to a high degree of perfection. As my first completed new building it was not a bad attempt. Of course, it was nowhere as good as Norman Foster's building nearby, which really bent the rules, and I had a lot still to learn. The Apple building had come in under budget and I knew I had been tricked by the cost consultant, who earned praise from the developer for saving money that I could have used on finishes or a better staircase.

I had worked closely with Jamie Troughton on the design of Canning Town Interchange station on Roland Paoletti's new Jubilee Line extension. With railway engineers in Troughton's family ancestry, he maintained an interest in rail-infrastructure projects that John McAslan did not. When Jamie returned to Scotland some years after I had joined, I became design director of the renamed John McAslan + Partners and worked in close proximity to the new technical director, Piers Smerin. We didn't work on the same projects but had been given responsibilities in the management of the practice, which was useful for the next chapter of my life.

Neither of us had given any thought to leaving our well-paid jobs and starting a new practice. I had worked there for eight years, had designed the Jubilee Line station, an operations centre for a bank in Istanbul and the headquarters for Max Mara in Reggio Emilia in Italy. One evening after work, I drove to Covent Garden to collect my wife from the Design Council's new offices in Bow Street – and she asked me to come in and meet John Sorrell, the Chairman of the Design Council, as he and his wife Frances were buying a house in Highgate and were interviewing architects. The next day, I mentioned my meeting to Piers to see if he would be interested in working on it with me. It was only when we had concluded that this was not a project the practice would be interested in that the prospect of establishing our own practice emerged. Having been interviewed by the Sorrells – who, it has to be said, had not at that point bought the house – we were offered the job and left McAslan's office for uncharted territory.

The project for John and Frances Sorrell and their sons was an opportunity to breathe new life into the 1950s house designed by the architect Leonard Manasseh, who had designed three dwellings on the site of an old Victorian house – including one for himself at the southern end, on the edge of Highgate Cemetery, in which he continued to live until he died in 2017. The bold concept to retain the simplified core of the 1950s house and build new glazed extensions to the front and sides, and to construct a fully glazed studio on the roof, was ambitious but found favour with the Camden planners even in the face of opposition from the Highgate Society.

Having carried my drawings of a glass house across the Atlantic and back as a student, I saw then that a variation of that early house concept was approaching realisation when planning consent was granted for the largely glazed building between two listed Georgian terraces in Highgate's Pond Square.

This was an important milestone for the practice and indeed for John and Frances, for whom the project was equally a manifesto – and, as Chairman of the Design Council, John Sorrell would have anticipated the attention that his own house would later receive. Surprisingly, we had not felt the pressure we were under at the time, but it was a vindication of our design and of the Sorrells' brave patronage of a new practice when this residential project was shortlisted for the Stirling Prize in 2001 alongside major projects including the Michael Hopkins parliamentary office building, Portcullis House. In its context, The Lawns was a radical intervention and the RIBA jury noted that it was an 'exemplar of how the 21st century house can be incorporated into historic conservation areas as part of the continuing evolution of domestic architecture'.

As I finally began to build, I became more aware of the challenges of executing buildings to the level of perfection that I imposed upon myself as much as on the contractors. For me, it was not enough for a great concept to exist on paper alone; the detail had to follow. Chasing perfection was in my DNA.

Not long after the completion of The Lawns, we were approached by the owner of a nearby house in Highgate Cemetery who had observed the construction of the Sorrell house and wanted a residence to surpass it. Having established that the existing steel house on the site, designed by the architect John Winter, could not be retained, I arranged to meet him and raise the subject of its demolition and replacement. As a post-war architect, Winter was instinctively pragmatic. He understood that a replacement was inevitable given the failing structural frame of the existing house and the high value of the site and its potential for development, asking only that the new building should be better than the existing. When he wrote a review of the house for *Architecture Today*, he was generous in his praise – writing about the new House in Highgate Cemetery, 'This comes as near to being a faultless building as I have seen for a long time'.

As an architect aware of the challenges of getting a house built to this quality, John Winter's review seemed to make my struggle worthwhile. And with each new project, I considered new ways of meeting the challenge of construction – specifying larger proportions of the building and interior to be manufactured in workshops off-site, and employing the skills of furniture makers and metalworkers to work to a greater degree of accuracy than the construction industry could.

One of my favourite street facades in this book is that of a house in Putney made from Cor-Ten steel and glass. I had taken a trip to Portobello Road one Saturday morning, winding in and out of the stalls and galleries browsing with very little aim other than to enjoy a rare morning doing very little. I encountered a stall almost entirely dedicated to silver cutlery and there in a bundle was a rare set of Georgian, silver three-pronged forks, characteristically undecorated and minimal in design. I soon became engaged in the esoterics of the subject with the friendly stallholders, and exchanged cards – the forks were beautiful but too expensive. Two weeks later, I received a call asking if I would be interested in designing a house for them. The house in Putney is one example of the unexpected source of architectural patronage. And for me, as a work of architecture it combines many of the design principles that underpin our practice's work – to respond imaginatively to the site context, to push the boundaries of planning and to create a home that resolves the issues of life that had led to commissioning us to design a new house in the first place. If all of these are criteria that would seem to be common to all projects, then it is perhaps the sculptural quality of a house that makes the art of architecture more enduring and significant in its context.

Since writing a piece for the *RIBA Journal* entitled 'Homes made to measure', I have become increasingly interested in patronage and its role historically in the evolution of domestic architecture.

In 1997, with the introduction of Planning Policy Guidance 7 (PPG7), it became possible to gain planning consent to build an isolated house in the countryside, if outstanding in terms of its architectural and landscape design – a judgement outsourced to the specialist Design Review Panels. Although not all Paragraph 80 applications constitute large tracts of land, the relationship between acreage and land use to sustain the main house and its associated structures is significant. It is this relationship that leads us to study the evolution of the country estate and its modern day form.

In the context of 'Unique Houses' it is the interpretation of the patron's individual brief that can lead to the widest of architectural responses, from modest intervention to more sculptural expression. Both are equally valid if they respond to the defining characteristics of the setting.

Over time, and considering clients' reactions to concept presentations, I have learned that there should always be a design option that will challenge the client's expectation. Design satisfies both functional requirements and, equally, emotional needs. Our role as architects is manifold, but above all I believe we have a responsibility to inspire. To get to this position, invariably we first have to produce the scheme that responds logically to the site and accommodates all the spaces in the brief. It is only at that point with the knowledge we have accumulated that we can throw it up in the air, start again and produce something exceptional.

The project for Greenways, a house in Coombe Park in Kingston, is located in a gated enclave relatively close to the centre of London. I had been invited to meet the owner and discuss the design of a new house to replace a modest, post-war bungalow on the site. I found out much later that I had been the worst at interview but nevertheless had been given the job. Over the course of the ten years we worked on the project together, we became very good friends. Unusually, it was one of those projects where the design appeared quite effortlessly on paper. It was that Hejduk moment when the forms, in this case derived from the existing landscape, found an immutable geometric resolution that could not be questioned by me or by the client. It was to be, and it was that concept that as a team we worked so hard to build without compromise. Sitting at the dining table of the Bluebird restaurant almost weekly, the client and I would discuss every single detail of the design, and his questioning led me to stand up for what I thought was absolutely the right way to do it or return with another option the following week if I failed to convince him and also myself. This is the closest of our projects so far to a Gesamtkunstwerk, translated literally as 'total work of art' – we were encouraged by the client to consider every detail of the building in the context of the overall concept, producing a consistency of detail throughout the house that included the design of bespoke door handles generated from the geometric plan form of the building. It was a process that we all enjoyed, as had been the client's intention at the outset – and in reward for the total commitment by the client and by our team, the project won the Manser Medal for the best house in the UK in 2017. Having been shortlisted twice before, we celebrated the success with the added satisfaction that credit had been bestowed on our client for his ambition and determination to create a building that the Modern House described as 'one of the finest and most original houses to have been built in London in the past decade', adding, 'Greenways is a sculptural masterpiece'.

Projects are successfully achieved through the coming together of a team of people who each contribute complementary skills – and, equally, we acknowledge the client's determination and commitment through the periods of design and construction.

I complete this afterword with an acknowledgement of all the clients, architects, designers, students and collaborators who have worked with the practice since 1998 and who have contributed a part of their lives to these projects. I hope that, in the same way in which I drew inspiration from the offices that I worked in when younger, the architects and students who have worked in our studio have in some way benefitted from their experience. I extend special thanks to the architect Mike Gibson, who joined me ten years ago and who has taken on the important responsibilities for the detailing and management of many of the houses illustrated in this book as well as the design of some of our more recent projects. I acknowledge, too, that anyone chasing perfection in architecture is not the easiest person to work with – but I do hope that when we look back on projects that clients have said exceeded their expectations, and that other architects and journalists have positively reviewed, then we can agree that it has all been worthwhile. I also thank my family for their endurance and continued support – and wish them to understand that when in architecture we talk about 'the team', they are part of that team too.

Nick Eldridge

# ELDRIDGE LONDON PRACTICE CHRONOLOGY

1998    Eldridge Smerin Founded

1999    BT Cellnet / O2 Mobile Applications Development Centre (completed)

2000    **House in Highgate – 'The Lawns'** (completed)

2001    Selfridges Birmingham (completed)
**House in Hampstead** (completed)
House in Pimlico (completed)
RIBA Award: The Lawns
RIBA Stirling Prize Finalist: The Lawns
Camden Design Awards: The Lawns
Civic Trust Award: The Lawns

2002    House in Highgate Hill (planning approved)
Villa Moda, Kuwait – luxury brands store interior and landscape (completed)

2003    House in Sion Hill, Bath (planning approved)
Paragraph 80 House in Kent (planning approved)
Malmains Manor (concept)
Oppenheimer & Sons (de Beers) offices (completed)

2004    Selfridges Birmingham, interior (completed)

2005    British Library Intellectual Property Centre (completed)
Apartment in Westminster (completed)
Design Council Offices (completed)
V&A Museum Breckman Room Sorrell Foundation Exhibition (completed)
Four Marketing – Fashion Headquarters, London (completed)
Shed Private Members Club, London (completed)

2006    House in Chichester (concept)
House in Hadley Wood (concept)
British Library Framework (completed)
Sorrell Foundation/Somerset House (completed)

2007    **House in Highgate Cemetery** (completed)
**House in Belsize Park** (completed)
Winkreative Offices (completed)
House in Battersea (planning approved)

2008    House in Pangbourne (planning approved)
Farnborough International Venue & Events (concept)
Potters Fields, Tower Bridge, London residential development (concept)

2009    House in Ulcombe, Kent (completed)
House in Osterley (concept)
Shakespeare's Globe Education Centre, Bankside, London (completed)
RIBA Award: House in Highgate Cemetery
RIBA Award: House in Belsize Park
RIBA London Building of the Year: Finalist
RIBA Stephen Lawrence Award: Finalist
RIBA Manser Medal / House of the Year: Finalist
BD Architect of the Year Winner

2010    **House in Epsom** (completed)

House in Chelsea (completed)
House in Farnham (concept)
Apartment in Pimlico (completed)

2011  House in Moscow (concept)
House in Chelsea (planning approved)
House in Fulham (completed)
Water Tower House (competition)
Peter Pears Gallery, Aldeburgh (concept)
RIBA Award: House in Epsom
BD Architect of the Year Finalist

2012  House in Twickenham (planning approved)
House on Hampstead Heath (concept)

2013  House in Battersea (completed)
House in South Kensington (planning approved)
Whitgift School, new science classrooms and biomes (planning approved)
Farmhouse in Surrey (concept)

2014  **House in Putney** (completed)
Mill conversion in Wiltshire (completed)
House in West Sussex (concept)
House in Chiswick (planning approved)

2015  **House in Chelsea** (completed)
House in Bohemia (competition)
Duplex Apartment in Highgate (completed)
Eldridge Smerin rebranded to Eldridge London

2016  House in Roehampton (planning approved)

2017  **House in Coombe Park** (completed)
House in Oxted (concept)
House in Devon (planning approved)
Mansion conversion in Hertfordshire (completed)

Manser Medal: House in Coombe Park
British Homes Awards, Large House of the Year: House in Coombe Park

2018  House in the Chilterns (concept)
**House in Notting Hill** (completed)
House in Greenwich (completed)
House in Penberth Cove (concept)
Eldridge Newlyn Established
BD Architect of the Year: Finalist

2019  Penthouse in Battersea (concept)
Country House in Oxfordshire, Competition
House in Salcombe
Heatherley School of Fine Art, London, Studios library and office extension
Longage Manor Farm Café, Spa & Residences (planning approved)

2020  Paragraph 80 House in Surrey Hills (concept)
Manor House in Ayrshire (concept)
**House & Studio in Cornwall** (completed)
Manor House in Kent (planning approved)

2021  **Garden House in Highgate** (completed)
**House in Shoreham by Sea** (completed)
Paragraph 80 House in Surrey (under construction)
Penthouse in Notting Hill (under construction)
House in Perranuthnoe, Cornwall (under construction)
*House & Garden* Top 100

2022  Paragraph 80 House in Wiltshire
House in Stockwell
BD Architect of the Year: Finalist

# INDEX

Illustrations and their captions are denoted by the use of *italic* page numbers.

Aalto, Alvar 47
Andre, Carl, *Equivalent VIII installation* 155
Apple, Stockley Park, West London 10–11, 166
Architectural Association (AA) 9, 163, 164–5
Arts and Crafts movement 72, 81
AT&T Building, Madison Avenue, Manhattan 9, 164

Bijvoet, Bernard 163
Blom, Jinny 114, 117, 130, 133
Blue Shark flatware (Slune) 7
Breuer, Marcel 75
Brûlé, Tyler 12
Business & Intellectual Property Centre, British Library 12

Canning Town Underground station 11, 166
Centre Pompidou, Paris 163
Chamberlin, Powell and Bon 8
Chareau, Pierre 163
Conservation Areas 7, 60, 109, 117, 141
Cook, Peter 165
Crosby, Theo 8, 164

Dalbet, Louis 163
Design Council 11, 100, 166
Design Review Panels 15, 168

Eldridge, Alison (wife) 10, 11–12, 166
Eldridge London 12
Eldridge Newlyn 12, 15, 152
Eldridge, Nick
background 7–9, 161–2
beginnings 9–11, 162–6
chasing perfection 161–9
independent practice 11–15, 166–9
plans
   Barn, Newlyn, Cornwall *151*
   Beach House, Shoreham-by-Sea *52–3*
   Cor-Ten House Putney, London *72–3*
   Garden House, Highgate, London *86–7*
   Greenways, Coombe Park, Kingston *22–3*
   House, Belsize Park, London *114–15*
   House, Chelsea, London *123*
   House, Epsom, Surrey *42–3*
   House, Hampstead, London *132–3*
   House, Highgate Cemetery, Highgate, London *62–3*
   House, Notting Hill, London *140*
   The Lawns, Highgate, London *102*
prizes
   Manser Medal 20, 34, 168
   RIBA Award 48, 69, 106
   shortlists
   London Building of the Year 69
   Manser Medal 48, 69, 168
   Stephen Lawrence Prize 69
   Stirling Prize 6, 12, 106
   themes and variations 16
works
   Barn, Newlyn, Cornwall 97, *148–59, 149–50, 153–4, 157–8*
   Barvikha House, Moscow 16
   Beach House, Shoreham-by-Sea 12, 50–7, *51, 53–5*
   Cor-Ten House Putney, London 60, 70–81, *71–2, 74, 76–80*, 167
   Garden House, Highgate, London 12, *17*, 82–95, *83–5, 88–90, 92–4*

Greenways, Coombe Park, Kingston 6, 7, 16, 19, 20–37, *21, 24–33, 36–7*, 86, 95, 159, 168

House, Belsize Park, London 97, 110–19, *111–13, 116, 119*

House, Chelsea, London 120–7, *121–2, 125–6*

House, Epsom, Surrey 19, 38–49, *39–41, 44–7, 49*

House, Hampstead, London 128–37, *129–31, 134, 136–7*

House, Highgate Cemetery, Highgate, London 6, *13*, 50, 58–69, *59–61, 63, 65–8*, 167

House, Notting Hill, London 138–47, *139, 141, 143–6*

The Lawns, Highgate, London 6, 11–12, *11*, 58, 97, 98–109, *99–100, 103–4, 107–9*, 166–7

Modular House (prefab) *14–15*, 15

Paragraph 80 House, Surrey Hills *14*, 15

Stilemans, Surrey 16

Eldridge Smerin 11–12

Elliott, Richard 58, 60, 61, 69

*Equivalent VIII* installation (Andre) 155

Esherick House, Pennsylvania 47

*Five Architects: Eisenman, Graves, Gwathmey, Hejduk, Meier* (1972) 165

Flatiron Building, New York 8, 164

Fletcher, Alan 8, 164

Fletcher Forbes Gill 8

Forbes, Colin 8, 164

Foster, Norman 9, 10, 165

Foster + Partners 9, 11

Frampton, Kenneth 165

France 10, 162, 163, 165

Frost, Terry, Through Blues 101, 148

Future Systems 9, 12

geodesic domes 9

*Gesamtkunstwerk* 34, 163, 168

Gibson, Mike 12, 169

works 142

Beach House, Shoreham-by-Sea 50, 53, 57

Garden House, Highgate, London 82, 86, 91, 95

Greenways, Coombe Park, Kingston 95

House, Notting Hill, London 138, 141

Glass House, New Canaan, Connecticut 9, 164

Goldfinger, Ernö 98

Grange, Kenneth 8

Greene & Greene 75

Grimshaw, Nicholas 10

Hadid, Zaha 11, 165

Hansen, Fritz 7, 161

Harben, Henry 114

Hejduk, John 165

Herron, Ron 9, 164, 165

High-tech architecture 10

Highgate and Hampstead houses 98

Highgate Cemetery *13, 59–61*, 60

Highgate Society 12, 166

Hong Kong 8, 10, 162

Hopkins House, Hampstead 8

Hopkins, Michael and Patty 7–8, 10, 98, 167

House 10 (Hejduk) 165

HSBC, Hong Kong 10

IBM Greenford 10, 165

Jacobsen, Arne 7

Japan 8, 72, 79, 81, 162–3

Jensen, Georg 7

Joe (joiner) 156

John Deere Headquarters, Moline, Illinois 70

Johnson, Philip 9, 16, 164

Kahn, Louis 47

Kaplický, Jan 9, 10, 12, 165

Lautner, John 34

Le Corbusier 162, 163, 164

Libeskind, Daniel 165

INDEX **173**

Liverpool 8, 9, 163, 164
London Building of the Year 69

McAslan, John 10–11, 166
McAslan + Partners 10–11, 12
Magna Centre, Rotherham 106
Maison de Verre, Paris 163
Manasseh, Leonard 98, 101, 109, 166
Manser Medal 20, 34, 48, 69, 168
Mason, Jim 20, 35
Médiathèque building (Carré d'Art), Nîmes 10, 165

New York 8–9
Newlyn School, The 148
Nicholson, Ben 152
Niemeyer, Oscar 34–5
North Carolina 8
Nouvel, Jean 10, 165

Ozenfant, Amédée 163

Palladio 162
Paoletti, Roland 166
Pearson, Dan 105
Pentagram 8, 9, 164
Perez, Charles and Seema 110, 114, 118
Piano, Renzo 163
Planning Policy Guidance 7 (PPG7) 168
Portcullis House, London 167
Price, Cedric 163
promenade architecturale 16, 30

Renault building, Swindon 9, 164–5
RIBA Award 48, 69, 106
Rietveld, Gerrit 163
Rogers, Richard 10, 163

Saarinen, Eero 70
St Ives, Cornwall 153, 155
Selfridges Birmingham 12
Shakespeare's Globe Theatre, Bankside 8

Shapero, Bernard and Emma 128, 130, 135
Shoreham Beach 50, 53
skyscrapers 9
Slune, Svend 7
Sorrell, John and Frances 11–12, 98, 100–1, 105–6, 109, 128, 148, 166–7
steel, weathered 70
Stephen Lawrence Prize 69
Stirling Prize 6, 12, 106
sustainability 15, 38, 48, 97, 109, 127, 155
Swains Lane, Highgate 58, 70, 82

tatami mat, Japanese 79, 81, 163
Through Blues (Frost) 148
trefoil motif 23, 26, 33, 34
Troughton, Jamie 10–11, 166
Troughton McAslan 165–6

Villa Mairea, Finland 47
Villa Moda department store, Kuwait 12

Whitney Museum of American Art, Manhattan 75
WilkinsonEyre 106
Winkreative 12
Winter, John 12, 60–1, 69, 70, 98, 167

# CREDITS

## PICTURE CREDITS

The publisher would like to thank the copyright holders for granting permission to reproduce the images illustrated. Every attempt has been made to trace accurate ownership of copyrighted images in this book. Any errors or omissions will be corrected in subsequent editions provided notification is sent to the publisher.

James Brittain: pages 121–226
Richard Davies: pages 99, 103–108
Lyndon Douglas: pages 13, 39–49, 59, 61–68, 74–76, 80–90, 93, 111–119, 129, 131–137
Nick Guttridge: pages 21–37, 71
Eldridge London: pages 14–15, 51, 54–55, 60, 77–79, 92, 94, 100, 130, 139–146. Model on page 15 by Stephen Setford
Eldridge Newlyn: pages 149–158
Andrew Putler: page 11
Christian Spencer-Davies: page 161. Model on page 161 by AMODELS

## ELDRIDGE LONDON STUDIO MEMBERS PAST AND PRESENT

Matt Atkins
Selim Bayer
Lucy Begg
Silvia Boev
Antje Bulthaup
Alex Cochrane
George Dawes
Ana Eusebio
Will Flint
Mike Gibson
Nicolo Giuriato
Richard Glover
Magdalena Gorska
Steven Harp
Natasha Ho
Inga Jonsdottir
Hiroki Kakizoe
Kamila Klimczac
Agnieszka Krawcyzk
Annette Leber
Karolina Malyska
Eleanora Massaccesi
Dominika Matusiak
Tom McGlynn
Ewa Pobudejska
Karin Poetscher
Alison Poole
Emilie Quesne
Sandra Robinson
Daisy Roth
Amalia Skoufoglou
Piers Smerin
Harry Sturge
Megumi Taguchi
Sonia Tomic
Kathi Weber
Kasia Wierzbicka
Daniel Wilson

First published in 2022 by Lund Humphries

Lund Humphries
Huckletree Shoreditch
Alphabeta Building
18 Finsbury Square
London, EC2A 1AH
www.lundhumphries.com

*Nick Eldridge: Unique Houses* © Dominic Bradbury, 2022

All rights reserved

978-1-84822-420-9

A Cataloguing-in-Publication record for this book is available from the British Library.
All rights reserved. No part of this publication may be reproduced, stored in a retrieval
System or transmitted in any form or by any means, electrical, mechanical or otherwise,
without first seeking the permission of the copyright owners and publishers. Every effort
has been made to seek permission to reproduce the images in this book. Any omissions
are entirely unintentional, and details should be addressed to the publishers.

Dominic Bradbury has asserted his right under the Copyright, Designs and Patent Act,
1988,to be identified as the Author of this Work.

Front and cover: Interior of Greenways, Coombe Park, Kingston
Back cover: Exterior of Greenways, Coombe Park, Kingston
Copy-edited by Ian McDonald
Designed by Myfanwy Vernon-Hunt, This-Side
Set in Untitled Sans, Klim Type Foundry
Printed in Belgium